WHEELS

the story of the automobile

by W. E. BUTTERWORTH

and PISTONS

FOUR WINDS PRESS/NEW YORK

Published by Four Winds Press
A Division of Scholastic Magazines, Inc., New York, N. Y.
Copyright © 1971 W. E. Butterworth
All Rights Reserved
Printed in the United States of America

Library of Congress Catalogue Card Number: 74-124190

This book is respectfully dedicated to the memory of a long departed 1927 Essex Opera Coupe, acquired by the author in 1945 when it was seventeen, two years older than he was.

The frame was bent so that it made right turns and long, sweeping left curves. It had a gravity fuel pump which required refilling every three miles, because the connection to the gasoline tank had long been severed. There was a hole in the floorboard through which rain, mud, and a good deal else could and did enter the passenger compartment. The roof consisted of a thick layer of Roof Seal and a thin layer of rotten wood. It had coil springs in the seats, most of them visible. It had only one door, and that was stuck shut, so I had to climb through the window. Downhill, it would make perhaps forty miles per hour.

But it was mine, all twenty-four dollars worth, and I was King of the Road.

Gone but not forgotten, thou good and faithful servant!

W. E. Butterworth

Fairhope, Alabama

CROSS SECTION, MODEL T

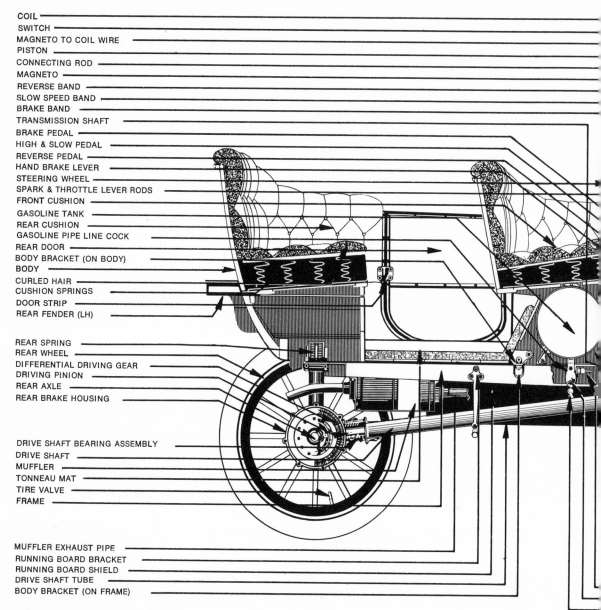

COIL
SWITCH
MAGNETO TO COIL WIRE
PISTON
CONNECTING ROD
MAGNETO
REVERSE BAND
SLOW SPEED BAND
BRAKE BAND
TRANSMISSION SHAFT
BRAKE PEDAL
HIGH & SLOW PEDAL
REVERSE PEDAL
HAND BRAKE LEVER
STEERING WHEEL
SPARK & THROTTLE LEVER RODS
FRONT CUSHION
GASOLINE TANK
REAR CUSHION
GASOLINE PIPE LINE COCK
REAR DOOR
BODY BRACKET (ON BODY)
BODY
CURLED HAIR
CUSHION SPRINGS
DOOR STRIP
REAR FENDER (LH)

REAR SPRING
REAR WHEEL
DIFFERENTIAL DRIVING GEAR
DRIVING PINION
REAR AXLE
REAR BRAKE HOUSING

DRIVE SHAFT BEARING ASSEMBLY
DRIVE SHAFT
MUFFLER
TONNEAU MAT
TIRE VALVE
FRAME

MUFFLER EXHAUST PIPE
RUNNING BOARD BRACKET
RUNNING BOARD SHIELD
DRIVE SHAFT TUBE
BODY BRACKET (ON FRAME)

The Model T—it put the world on wheels. FORD ARCHIVES

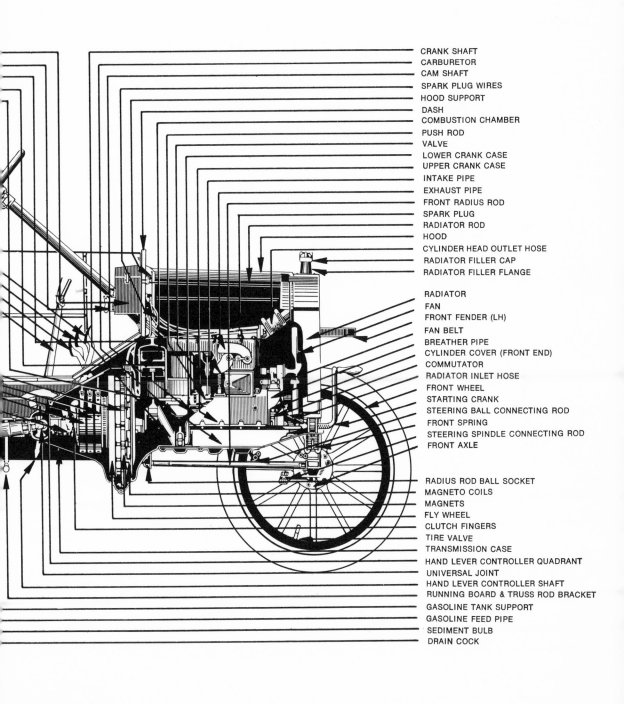

CRANK SHAFT
CARBURETOR
CAM SHAFT
SPARK PLUG WIRES
HOOD SUPPORT
DASH
COMBUSTION CHAMBER
PUSH ROD
VALVE
LOWER CRANK CASE
UPPER CRANK CASE
INTAKE PIPE
EXHAUST PIPE
FRONT RADIUS ROD
SPARK PLUG
RADIATOR ROD
HOOD
CYLINDER HEAD OUTLET HOSE
RADIATOR FILLER CAP
RADIATOR FILLER FLANGE

RADIATOR
FAN
FRONT FENDER (LH)
FAN BELT
BREATHER PIPE
CYLINDER COVER (FRONT END)
COMMUTATOR
RADIATOR INLET HOSE
FRONT WHEEL
STARTING CRANK
STEERING BALL CONNECTING ROD
FRONT SPRING
STEERING SPINDLE CONNECTING ROD
FRONT AXLE

RADIUS ROD BALL SOCKET
MAGNETO COILS
MAGNETS
FLY WHEEL
CLUTCH FINGERS
TIRE VALVE
TRANSMISSION CASE
HAND LEVER CONTROLLER QUADRANT
UNIVERSAL JOINT
HAND LEVER CONTROLLER SHAFT
RUNNING BOARD & TRUSS ROD BRACKET
GASOLINE TANK SUPPORT
GASOLINE FEED PIPE
SEDIMENT BULB
DRAIN COCK

It seems to be an unfortunate fact of life that man is at his inventive best when he is motivated by the thought of doing grievous bodily harm to his fellows. The atom bomb comes immediately to mind, of course, in this connection, but long before this came the first self-propelled road vehicle.

CHAPTER I

At the time, 1769, George Washington was a loyal subject of His Majesty the King. Washington's major interests were his still, his 15,000-acre plantation, Mount Vernon, and his own wild idea of transportation—raising mules when everybody said that it couldn't be done.

In France, a relatively obscure Captain of Artillery, one Nicholas Joseph Cugnot, had an idea even more absurd than breeding mules. He was building a machine to haul cannon, a machine he announced would do away with the horse and make French artillery absolutely invincible.

Cugnot was going to harness the power of steam, to make it turn a wheel, and when the wheel turned, to pull behind it a cannon. He was building a locomotive, or an automobile, a self-propelled vehicle.

The fact that George Washington, the Virginia planter, was the first successful breeder of mules in the Colonies has been obscured by his other later accomplishments. Captain Cugnot is remembered as the father of the automobile.

It was at once very simple and very large and ungainly. It consisted of a tricycle, with the single wheel forward serving as the driving wheel. Mounted ahead of the driving wheel was the boiler. When a coal fire had generated enough steam pressure, the steam was released to pistons on either side of the driving wheel. As one piston was forced down, the other was forced up. A hook engaged a lug on the side of the wheel, pulling it upward and the wheel forward.

It worked. On the miserable roads of the day, it moved forward at the incredible speed of two and a half miles per hour, including the time required to stop every several hundred feet to get steam pressure up again.

Captain Cugnot was faced with very much the same problems that plague the engineers of Ford and Chrysler and Mercedes and Rolls-Royce today. He had a problem of traction. The driving wheel would sometimes slip on wet roads, spinning uselessly. He had steering problems. He had fuel-consumption problems. He had problems of weight and balance and of maintenance and lubrication. And he had the major problem that has bothered all inventors: a lack of understanding and financial support from a large block of influential people who considered what he was doing a shameful waste of time and money.

Cugnot's idea, however, inspired other people to try. Some of their experiments proved disastrous, and they all came up against what appeared to be an insoluble problem. The conversion of coal energy required so huge a vehicle that over-the-road travel was out of the question. The obvious solution was the railroad.

It made far better sense to develop a system of transportation where *one* steam engine could pull any number

10

Captain Cugnot's steam-driven carriage. BROWN BROTHERS

Trevithick's Steam Carriage of 1810. CULVER

of cars carrying hundreds of people at once. The rails of the railroad eliminated all steering problems. The man in charge of the engine, the engineer, had to worry only about keeping the boiler fueled up, not about making turns. Fuel consumption was such that it was necessary to haul a carload of fuel behind the engine.

The French, priding themselves on being practical, just about gave up on the idea of a personal over-the-road self-propelled vehicle and devoted themselves to the perfection of the railroad.

Across the English Channel, the British decided that there just might be a need for a locomotive, or automobile, to run along existing roads, rather than on rails. Their thinking probably was based in part on the need for transportation in India, and their other possessions, where labor was very cheap. Roads, in other words, could be built for the cost of labor alone, whereas railroads required large amounts of iron rails.

About thirty years after Captain Cugnot's artillery puller had first puffed down the road, a British engineer, Richard Trevithick, built a steam road carriage. It had four wheels, the two wheels in front being half the size of the two in the rear. A steering stick was connected to the small wheels, and the "conductor" (one who conducts, befitting the dignity of a self-propelled vehicle) sat in front.

There was an "engineer," charged with keeping the coal fire under the boiler burning. He rode in back, standing on a little platform. The Trevithick Steam Carriage spun a flywheel for inertial power, driving the driving wheels through gears.

It was a sound idea, and Trevithick in his later years became one of the most highly regarded railroad engineers; however, he was ahead of his time. After a few demonstration runs in and around London, his money ran out, and he couldn't find anyone to finance him. Finally he went broke and the steam road carriage was dismantled.

About twenty years later, in the 1820's, a man with the remarkably appropriate name of Goldsworthy Gurney did, at least for a time, make a financial success of his steam carriage. Gurney's operation was well-financed, mostly through the efforts of Sir Charles Dance. For a time, they actually made a profit from running steam carriages over stagecoach roads.

Goldsworthy Gurney drove his carriage in much the same way that even the late model steam engines were driven. Two cylinders were mounted parallel to the length of his carriage. Steam, generated in a boiler above, was fed to them. Their pistons were connected to cranks on the rear-axle shaft. When the pistons moved, they moved the axle, and thus the wheels. The only basic difference between Goldsworthy Gurney's power train and that of a more modern steam locomotive is that modern steam engines mount the pistons on either side of the chassis and connect the driving rod to the wheel itself, rather than the axle.

The initial success of Goldsworthy Gurney and Sir

Goldsworthy Gurney's steam carriage, patented in 1828. BROWN BROTHERS

Walter Hancock ran this steam carriage as part of the
London-Paddington Steam Carriage Company. BROWN BROTHERS

Charles Dance inspired two other partnerships in the business of over-the-road steam carriages. Maceroni and Squire as well as Summers and Ogle copied the horizontal-cylinder method of driving the wheels, but each developed their own boiler systems.

Gurney and Dance's boiler consisted of two boilers mounted across the carriage, one on top of the other. It was difficult to maintain steam pressure, even with a forced draught of the coal fire, because there wasn't very much surface to be heated. Maceroni and Squire developed a boiler, occupying just about the same amount of space, but made up of eighty thin vertical tubes, offering much more area for the fire to heat. Summers and Ogle's boiler only had thirty such tubes. Both improved boilers offered about two hundred fifty square feet of boiler surface to be heated, and both were much more efficient than Goldsworthy Gurney's two tubular boilers.

These were large vehicles, carrying eight to ten passengers, plus the conductor and the engineer. They generally moved at about 10 mph, but when the road was straight enough and level enough, they were capable of 30 mph. They operated on about two hundred pounds per square inch of steam pressure and weighed almost five thousand pounds each. In comparison, a full-sized 1969 Ford weighs 3,717 pounds and carries only six people. The Gurney and Dance steam carriage required about four-pence (eight cents) worth of coke per mile, and the improved boilers about six cents' worth. Since the U. S. Internal Revenue Service permits a business deduction of ten cents per mile for the use of a car, one might say that the steam carriages of one hundred eighty years ago were cheaper to run. Of course, they didn't go nearly as fast, nor as smoothly, and required a good half hour to get up steam.

Between 1828 and 1838, another Englishman, Walter Hancock, went into the steam carriage business. He started where the others had left off, learning from their mistakes, adding his own ideas, and coming up with a vastly improved road vehicle.

Hancock, by using flat tanks (called "water bags") in his boiler, instead of tubes or cylinders, developed an engine producing eighteen effective horsepower and occupying only 11.1 cubic feet of space (30 by 20 by 32 inches).

At one time Hancock had six carriages in operation at once, all carrying paying passengers on a regular schedule. He fastened his engine at the rear of the vehicle, the steam coming out of the top of the boiler and into a cylinder mounted perpendicularly. As the piston and the drive rod moved up-and-down, they turned a gear, the gear drove a chain, and the chain turned the rear wheels.

In 1830, Hancock invented an improved wheel, variations of which can still be seen on some horse-drawn, and even gasoline or steam-powered, wheels. He set sixteen spokes around the circumference of a wheel, each of them tapered on two radii so that when they were assembled, they formed a perfect circle of great strength.

Experiments were even conducted with a new product from the Colonies called rubber. It was theorized that if

16

a tube of this rubber substance could be filled with air, and then mounted on the outside of Hancock's wheel, some of the bumps in the road could be smoothed over.

In other words, a great deal was accomplished in the development of steam carriages in a relatively short period of time. It is interesting to speculate about what might have happened to steam carriages if their development had been continued.

But their development was stopped abruptly. The more the over-the-road steam carriage was improved, the greater the threat it posed to the steam railroads. The railroads had enough sense to realize this. An anti-steam-carriage program was initiated, skillfully playing on people's fears and self-interest. "Save our roads for horses!" was one cry. "Dangerous and dirty," was another.

In the late 1850's, the railroad interests won out. Parliament passed a "Locomotives on Highways Act." It protected the public interest by requiring that every "road locomotive" have "three persons in attendance," one of whom had to walk sixty yards ahead of the vehicle, carrying a red lantern at night, and a flag in the day time. The same act limited the speed of "road locomotives" to four miles per hour in the country and two miles in town.

At the same time, it must be admitted that the railroad had given the public cheap, reliable, transportation between cities. Transportation within cities, by horsedrawn wagon or trolley, was cheaper than the steam carriages. They died out, although a man named J. Scott Russell refused to quit and ran his steam carriage as late as 1857.

CHAPTER **II** It's very difficult for anyone, particularly an American, who is mobile from the time he first learns to roller-skate or ride a bicycle, to really understand how little mobility people had a hundred years ago.

There were three methods of transportation. The first was the horse. People could ride either on horseback, or in a horse-drawn vehicle of some kind, either a wagon in the country, or a trolley car in the few cities which had that modern convenience. Second, the steam locomotive, which carried people between cities, and in a few cases, within cities. Third, there was the bicycle. The bicycle was then (and remains in many parts of the world) an important, and often the only, means of transportation.

As it is difficult for the American teen-ager to imagine his father going off to the office or the plant on a bicycle, it is equally difficult for a teen-ager in, say Tokyo or Berlin, to imagine himself driving to high school in his own car, or even his parents' car.

Horses, like limousines, were simply beyond the means of the average Frenchman, or the average Englishman or German. They were expensive to buy, and then they had to be quartered, fed, shod, and cared for.

When, in the 1860's, the *velocipede* (literally, "fast foot") was invented, it was a major step in making man's life easier, even if it was ungainly and slow and rather ugly. It permitted man to go much faster than he had ever been able to go before, except by railroad or horse. More important, it gave him the chance (once the velocipede was paid for) to go at very little cost, at his own pace, and when he wanted to.

18

The velocipede was an ungainly monster, with a heavy wooden frame and wooden wheels. The rider sat on a bar between the front and rear wheels, and propelled himself along by pushing with his feet. It wasn't fast, and it wasn't what the physicists would call an efficient use of energy, but it was certainly faster than walking. When the rider pushed himself to the top of a hill, he could roll down the other side. That was a remarkable and wonderful improvement to people used to walking down hills as well as up them.

Within twenty years, by the 1880's, the velocipede had evolved into an even more amazing manifestation of man's inventive genius, the "ordinary bicycle," which was very different from the bicycle we know today. In England, it was called the *"penny-farthing,"* because its two wheels bore roughly the same relationship to each other in size as did the penny and the farthing. The front wheel was huge, with a radius equal the length of a man's legs. He rode on top of the front wheel, and his feet, instead of pushing on the ground, pushed on pedals. A tubular framework held a steering bar (called a handlebar in the United States) and a very small rear wheel.

There were no gears. The rider with his leg muscles had to provide whatever effort was required to turn the large wheel. Neither were there brakes. Balance was difficult, and a spill was a spill indeed. But it was a grand and glorious feeling for the rider of a bicycle, who had never believed that he would be able to go any faster than his feet would carry him, to go sailing down a street, passing the pedestrians and even horses.

After some false starts, the self-propelled vehicle evolved from the "ordinary" into the "safety bicycle." Tricycles were tried, but were not very successful. Women, of course, could not ride ordinarys, because their skirts kept them from straddling the wheel. The safety bicycle was the obvious answer. It incorporated the two-wheel idea of the velocipede, with the pedals and tubular frame of the ordinary, and permitted the rider to ride between the wheels. Pneumatic tires soon followed. Riding a bicycle became a perfectly natural thing for a woman to do.

The bicycle is significant for other reasons too. A little freedom, like a little knowledge, is sometimes a dangerous thing. The average Frenchman, or German, or Englishman, having been given the freedom of the bicycle, quite naturally wanted something a little better.

It was a dream, of course, but there was no harm in dreaming. A rider then thought: Wouldn't it be nice if sometime 'they' could adapt an engine to fit a bicycle, so that all I would have to do is go along for the ride, rather than push pedals?

Wouldn't it be nice to be able to go wherever I wanted to go, paying no attention to schedules or fares?

Steam engines obviously were not going to replace the bicycle. They were simply too large. Internal-combustion engines weren't much smaller, but it seemed possible that they could be made small enough to propel a bicycle, or a small, horseless carriage.

The idea of the internal-combustion engine was not new. It differed only from the steam engine in that the piston driving force was generated inside the cylinder, instead of outside, and then put into the cylinder. A gun (and guns were certainly common enough) was a form of the internal-combustion engine. Powder inside the barrel was ignited, and converted to gas, and when it expanded, it forced the bullet out the end of the barrel. Only two things were required: First, a replacement for gun powder, which could be metered into the cylinder as often, and as rapidly, as necessary. Gas, and some sort of valving system, were the obvious solution to that problem. Second, some method of converting the velocity of the bullet/piston to practical use was needed; a method that would enable the piston to be used again and again.

When the "Locomotives on Highways Act" in England had efficiently stifled British development, France became the center of development for both road vehicles and power plants.

In 1860, Etienne Lenoir developed the first commercially successful internal-combustion engine. It was simplicity itself. It consisted of a cylinder and a piston, a piston rod, a crankshaft, and a flywheel.

Gas vapor was fed into the cylinder through holes in the cylinder wall. It ignited, and the force pushed the piston downward in the cylinder. The intake ports were closed by the movement of the piston. At the bottom of the stroke, the gases were exhausted through a set of exhaust ports. The inertia of the flywheel pushed the piston back up past the intake ports, more gas vapor entered the cylinder, and the cycle repeated.

It was almost as inefficient as it was simple. But it worked, and it became a success because it represented a convenient source of power which required no stoker for a coal fire, no water supply, and no boiler.

In Deutz, Germany, the firm of Otto and Langen took a good look at the Lenoir Engine, and told one of their employees, Gottlieb Daimler, to go ahead with his idea of a better, four-stroke, internal-combustion engine.

This too was a crude and inefficient engine, but it was so much of an improvement, and so much quieter in operation, that in 1876, the Otto Silent Gas Engine was almost an instant success.

The Daimler-designed Otto Silent Gas Engine turned a magnificent one hundred twenty revolutions per minute, and the "gas" meant just that—not gasoline or any other vaporized liquid. It was fueled by the same gas that provided illumination.

Six years after the engine was put into production, Daimler had a row with Otto and Langen and quit. Although they had no legal obligation to do anything, Otto and Langen settled a sum of money on him in appreciation of his work for the firm. It wasn't a fortune, but it was enough to permit Daimler to move to Cannstadt and set up a workshop in his back yard.

Their disagreement had been over the future of the internal-combustion engine. Otto and Langen wanted to continue with stationary engines. In other words, they wanted Daimler to devote his ability to the improvement of what he had already designed: a good, solid, reliable

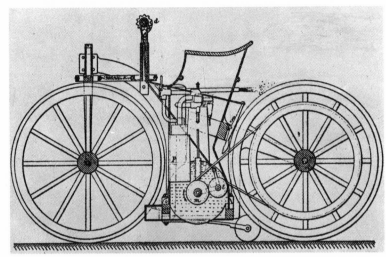

Daimler tried out this motor on a bicycle in 1885. CULVER

power source for factories. Daimler thought that the future of the internal-combustion engine lay with mobility. Given the time and opportunity, he believed that he could develop an engine which would be: (a) much lighter, (b) much more powerful because it would be much faster (turn higher rpm), and (c) be powered by fuel vapor, so that it could take its power supply with it.

Such an engine, Daimler announced, would have a ready market in the railroads, where it could be used to power light cars; in cities, where firemen could mount it on the back of a fire truck, and use it to power the pumps necessary to throw water on fires; and in boats, both as auxiliary power for the barges on the European canals and in pleasure boats. Admitting that it was rather

23

stretching the point, he even suggested that it might be possible for a light, high-speed internal-combustion engine to propel bicycles or carriages.

When Daimler left, he took with him his right-hand man, Wilhelm Maybach. A year later, Daimler and Maybach patented their first engine. Incidentally, while Daimler's name is fairly well-known in the United States, Maybach's isn't. In Europe, however, it's as well-known as that of Ransom Eli Olds or Francis Kettering, and Maybach trucks are as common as White or Reo trucks are in this country.

Their engine operated from fuel vapor. Gasoline was then a by-product, rather than the major product of the petro-chemical industry, and oddly enough, it was as powerful a fuel (in terms of octane rating) as present-day high-test gas. First the tank was filled with gasoline. Then air was drawn across the surface of the fuel to form a vapor, and the vapor was pulled into the combustion chamber.

The Daimler-Maybach "hot-tube" ignition system was clever and simple. A hollowed-out platinum bolt, closed at the outer end, was screwed into the cylinder at the combustion chamber. The outer, closed end was heated red-hot by an oil flame. Enough heat was conducted by the platinum to the interior of the tube to ignite the fuel vapor. After ignition, enough burned gas vapor remained inside the tube to prevent ignition for the next cycle until the piston, at the top of the compression cycle, overcame the pressure of the burned gas. This method of ignition had two advantages. For one thing, it was self-timing, providing "spark" (actually, ignition temperature) whenever, and only whenever, it was needed. For another, it did away with the only alternative available then, providing a spark by using electrical energy from batteries.

The first Daimler engine, like the Otto Silent Gas Engine, was horizontal; that is, the piston was parallel to the ground. Two years later, in 1865, Daimler and Maybach designed and built the first vertical gasoline internal-combustion engine. The 1865 engine enclosed the crankcase, the piston rod and the flywheel, the enclosure incorporating an oil reservoir for lubrication as well. The hot tube was heated by the same fuel as the engine consumed. And it turned over at a rate five times faster than the Otto Silent Gas Engine, an awe-inspiring six hundred revolutions per minute. It was about two and a half feet tall, weighed about one hundred ten pounds and generated a full half-horsepower.

For comparison, the Otto Silent Gas Engine weighed over two thousand pounds and was about seven feet high.

Daimler and Maybach experimented with vehicular use of their new engine, but its primary application was that of a lighter, smaller stationary engine. Within the next couple of years, however, they developed a 1.5 hp engine which proved that it could, on a level road, propel a carriage carrying four people at the dizzy speed of 10 mph.

At just about the same time, a man named Carl Benz, independently of Daimler, was in the process of developing his own engine and self-propelled vehicles. Benz had a small, but successful, business in Mannheim, which manufactured an electrically ignited two-cycle engine. In 1884, the courts decided that the four-cycle system, invented by Daimler and patented by Otto and Langen, had really been first patented by a Frenchman, Beau de Rochas, some ten years earlier. Rochas' four-cycle engine was unsuccessful, but since his idea had come first, the Otto and Langen patent was destroyed.

Benz was thus free to try his version of an engine following the four-cycle theory. In 1885 he built a one-cylinder engine with a 90-mm piston moving through a 150-mm stroke. It had (for the time) a high compression ratio of nearly 3:1 and developed 0.8 hp at 400 rpm. The Benz engine ignited the fuel by a spark from a coil connected to a battery. It was water-cooled (the unpleasant fact that high speed invariably means high temperature already having come up), but there was no radiator. It had a water tank, feeding water to water jackets, but the water was simply allowed to boil way.

Showing its stationary-engine ancestry, the Benz crank, connecting rod, and valves were exposed. The crank and connecting rod were greased with oil cups as stationary engines were traditionally greased. This engine had the same sort of rudimentary carburetion: Air was drawn across the surface of the fuel in the tank, forming a vapor.

Benz mated his engine to a tricycle in the same year. He attached it in the rear, with the flywheel horizontal and the crankshaft perpendicular. The first version had only one speed, but his .75 h.p. engine moved the car at a top speed of 9 mph. There were limitations to this performance. As often as not, when starting, the inertia of the car's weight was too much for the engine, which stalled. It would also stall on very slight grades.

The important thing, however, was that it ran at all. The idea was sound, and what was wrong could be improved. Within two years, Benz built a vehicle which had a two-speed transmission (leather belt driven, and obviously copied from the power trains of plant machinery of the day), larger tanks for the water to cool the engine, wooden wheels to replace wire-spoked ones, and brakes, because he now had a car which would not only go up hills with a 1:10 gradient, but reach speeds of 13 mph.

But, in the opinion of most solid Mannheimer burghers, the car was a waste of time, effort, and money for someone of Benz' obvious talents. Only his wife seemed to agree that not only did he have a good idea, but also one which might make him a good deal of money.

Benz dipped further into his bankroll and took his car to the Paris Exposition of 1887. It should be understood that Benz wasn't really bringing the firm to the brink of disaster by spending his money on the car. A closer comparison might be if a successful restaurant owner suddenly decided to go into the farming business himself, convinced that he would be able to grow better vegetables. It didn't make sense, but on the other hand, it was, after all, his money. Aside from giving him an earful of friendly advice, there wasn't much that anyone could do about his folly.

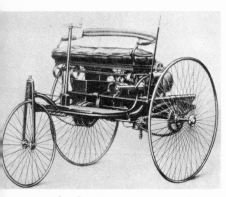

The first Benz car—actually a tricycle—built in 1885.

The Benz car was not the sensation of the Paris Exposition of 1887. It wasn't the first road vehicle the people had seen, and there didn't seem to be any world-shaking innovations in this particular horseless carriage. Benz was impassive. He returned to Mannheim no less encouraged or discouraged than he had been before.

A few weeks later, a French customer of Benz' stationary engines, who had not gone to the Exposition, heard about the Benz automobile. He got on the train to Frankfurt, transferred to the Mannheim train, showed up at the plant, and without further ado, put in an order for a Benz.

Neither Carl Benz, the seller, nor Emile Roger, the buyer, were wild-eyed dreamers. They were both successful businessmen. Benz proposed to Roger that he give him the exclusive franchise for Benz cars in all of France. Roger countered with a proposal that, in addition to selling Benz cars in France, he be licensed to assemble them in his shops in Paris. An agreement was drawn up, hands were shaken, and it is entirely possible that the two solemnized the agreement with a glass of brandy and a cigar. At that moment, although only Herr Benz and Monsieur Roger believed it, the automobile industry was born.

Business did not boom, but thanks mainly to stationary engines, neither did Benz wind up in bankruptcy court. In 1891, recognizing that a tricycle had a tendency to turn over on corners, Benz made a four-wheel version of his car. He redesigned the engine, replacing the large horizontal flywheel with a smaller one which turned in the

28

Benz built this four-wheel version of his car in 1891.
THE BETTMAN ARCHIVE, INC.

The Benz car of 1887, shown at the Paris Exposition. Benz is driving, and a partner, Max Rose, is in the passenger seat.
BROWN BROTHERS

perpendicular plane, and he increased the revolutions per minute to seven hundred.

By 1898, at the time of the Spanish-American War, Benz had a 9 hp car, capable of making twenty-five miles an hour. This car was an improved model of the first four-wheeler, rather than an entirely new design. Benz was the first advocate of improving an existing model, rather than starting fresh over and over again.

He was also the first advocate, before Ford, of the idea that the automobile belonged to everyone as a means of transportation, rather than seeing it as one more expensive toy for the rich. He was subjected to some ridicule for this too, especially by his French competitors.

The most important Frenchman in the automotive field then was Emile Levassor, of the firm of Panhard *et* Levassor, of Paris. He agreed with Benz and Daimler that the automobile was the coming thing. He didn't think much of the Roger-Benz, the French assembled Benz, nor of the Daimler-Maybach car, which he took the trouble to see in Cannstadt in 1890.

A year later, Levassor built his first car. He bought an engine from Gottlieb Daimler, a startling innovation of two cylinders placed in a V. This idea was to tantalize engine designers for years, until they were finally able to make it work. Levassor mounted this first V-2 precisely in the middle of his chassis. Then he mounted two seats, back to back, over it. No sooner was it completed than he began to modify it, so that no one now is quite sure which of the versions came first. Then, apparently deciding that a fresh start was called for, he scrapped his first car and built his second.

This was really a radical vehicle. Instead of mounting the engine in back where it belonged, or, in the exact center of the car where he had put it before, he put it out in front of the driver. Moreover, instead of mounting the engine so that the crankshaft was parallel with the axles, making transfer of power very simple, he mounted it with the crankshaft down the center line of the car.

This posed the problem of getting the power from the crankshaft, which was revolving around the center line, to the wheels, which had to turn at right angles to the center line. Although a phalanx of well meaning advisors insisted that bevel gears would not work, Levassor said that bevel gears were the only answer—especially for the future where engines of as many as 30, 35 or even 50 hp were entirely possible.

In the final version of the Panhard-Levassor car, power was transmitted from the engine through a friction clutch (operated by a foot lever) to a drive shaft, to a differential, and finally, via bevel gears, to chains which turned the rear wheels.

The car had a three-speed transmission, and an impressive array of controls. Steering was by a lever, which moved the front wheels. It had a dual-braking system. A hand lever, when pulled, applied brakes to the rear wheels and simultaneously disengaged the clutch. (Like all other cars of the day, Levassor's was driven according to the principle that the faster one could get the engine

The first Daimler car of 1886, with Daimler in the rear seat. BROWN BROTHERS

The Panhard-Levassor car for two passengers, and for four passengers.
Note that the engine is mounted ahead of the driver.   CULVER

to run, the better. It was therefore operated at a constant speed. Unless the engine was disconnected from the wheels when the brakes were applied, the brakes would have to work against the engine as well as against inertia.) A foot pedal, when pushed, would apply a brake to the driveshaft and at the same time disconnect the clutch. A second lever selected one of the three available transmission modes: forward, reverse, and neutral. A third lever selected the desired speed: first, second, and high. It was possible to go as fast in reverse as it was to go forward.

At first, the only control of engine speed was by a "governor," which kept the engine from turning more than 700–750 rpm's. Like many other engine parts, Levassor's governor was copied from stationary-engine parts. It worked on centrifugal force, with weighted balls revolving around a center column. When speed reached the desired maximum, the design of the governor was such that the balls' path kept the exhaust valves from opening, and the engine was more or less smothered by burned vapor until the speed and the path of the balls dropped, and the valves opened again.

The driver had a control on the dash, a crank-and-screw device, which moved the governor out of the way and permitted the engine to turn faster.

Sometime during the late 1890's, the crank-turning-a-screw was replaced with a spring-loaded foot pedal. When the pedal was pressed, the governor was disengaged, and the engine permitted to run faster. This pedal-operated lever was aptly christened the "accelerator."

The *Système Panhard,* in other words, had very much the controls and design of a present day "stick-shift" automobile or truck. But it was quite primitive. Levassor himself described it as "brutal."

Synchromesh gears were a long time from being invented. The gear connected to the engine very rarely, if ever, turned at the same speed as the transmission gear. Whenever gears were shifted and the clutch engaged, there was a violent jolt to the power train as the gear was either abruptly put into motion, or slowed down.

On the other hand, they were built to stationary-engine standards. They were designed and built to last a long time, no matter how much they tried to jar or shake themselves apart. One of the very first Panhard-Levassor cars, sold in the fall of 1891, proved how well they were built. It was still in use by a priest in the country when France went to war with Germany in 1914.

When it came to the automobile, the French government was very responsive to the mood of the people, and the mood of the people was that there should be no French restrictions, like the British "Locomotives on Highways Act" to restrain French inventiveness in this new grand adventure. The United States at the time (the Spanish-American War was to change this) regarded itself as sort of an independent colony. It was independent, but it was, or so most people seemed to think, still very much the primitive frontier. Science seemed to belong in Europe, and who could deny that the autocar was the ultimate in scientific development?

In 1895, Levassor built a car using a new Daimler engine. Instead of placing the cylinders in a V, Daimler had put them one behind the other. After a few test drives, Levassor proved that both he and the car were remarkably powerful and reliable by driving, without relief, for forty-eight hours and forty minutes on a 732-mile course, Paris-Bordeaux-Paris. His average speed was an incredible fifteen miles per hour!

Part of the success of the Daimler-powered Panhard-Levassor was credited to a new fueling device, developed by Maybach of the Daimler firm. Instead of relying on the natural, or forced, vaporization of fuel in a tank to get the fuel mixture to the cylinders, Maybach developed a part, called the carburetor, which sprayed the gas from jets.

The next year, the Panhards were fitted with cooling radiators, at first mounted on the rear, and then in front.

CHAPTER III

35

They were still inefficient, as only its own natural movement carried the heated water from the engine to the radiator to the reservoir. But they represented a major improvement over the old system, in which water heated by engine friction was simply permitted to boil away.

In the Paris-Marseilles Race of 1896, Levassor had a serious wreck, giving him internal injuries from which he died in 1897. The cause of the wreck was the tiller-steering arrangement. At high speeds (now over 20 mph), the direct-movement tiller mechanism was unsatisfactory. Levassor "oversteered." The car turned over and crushed him beneath it. In 1897, shortly after Levassor had died, the Panhard-Levassor came out with a steering wheel connected to a worm gear.

Several hundred self-propelled road vehicles actually were built in France around the turn of the century, and several thousand more were designed and proposed. Of those built, the vast majority were failures, but there were some conspicuous successes, and some which fell somewhere in between.

An American of some wealth, a man named Gardner, put a great deal of money into the firm of Leon Serpollet, who thought that steam power showed far more promise than the "internal-explosion" engine. There is a tendency to regard the steam-propelled car in the same light as the perpetual-motion machine, a strange and utterly useless vehicle dreamed up and driven by wild-eyed madmen.

The reverse is almost true. The steam engine then was tried and proven. It offered a great deal of power and a method of delivering that power to the wheels that was far superior to the gear-stripping jolting of the geared transmission. The steam engine made much less noise, and it generated its power without the stench and smoke of the gasoline engine.

Bad luck, more than anything else, caused the internal-combustion engine to pull alongside, and then outdistance the steam engine. The history of the steam-propelled automobile is full of second-place spots in races and endurance contests (as well, of course, as a number of spectacular wins). The steam cars seemed to have a perverse ability to fail several hundred yards from the finish line, to stop a hundred yards shy of the top of the hill in a hill climb, or to permit what the steamers called (with more than a little justification) "the stinking gas cars" to win the race and get the headlines. Second place simply was not good enough to attract people to buy cars, or to induce bankers to lend money for making improvements or beginning production.

Peugeot, for example, one of the early names in automobile manufacturing, began with a steam car. The firm of *Peugeot Frères* was a successful iron-working operation. One of the sons and nephews, Armand Peugeot, went to England, learned how to build bicycles, and then talked his father and his uncles into entering the bicycle business. When that proved successful, *Peugeot Frères* were willing to go along with Armand when he announced that, together with the American-financed Serpollet, he intended to build a steam-powered horseless carriage.

In the spring of 1890, the Peugeot-Serpollet Steam

A four-wheel Peugeot with a 3¼ hp gasoline engine. BROWN BROTHERS

Tricycle started out to prove itself on a well-publicized three-hundred-mile jaunt from Paris to Lyons. The engine was new, an adaptation of Serpollet's "instant-steam" flash boiler. It was a sound idea, and flash boilers have since become known for reliability and power.

On the three hundred miles, everything that could break, or leak, or come loose, broke, leaked, and came loose. It took five and a half days to make the three hundred miles. Something had to be blamed, and the Serpollet steam engine was elected.

The next Peugeot vehicle had four wheels and a Panhard–Levassor/Daimler gasoline engine.

A French aristocrat, Count Albert de Dion, quite early became as interested in the automobile as he was in the ladies, the horses, the card table, and food. Mainly because of his interest in the ladies and the card table, De Dion already had a reputation as a *duelliste* when in 1881, he decided that he would become an *automobiliste*. He thought of himself as a man of ideas, and not at all the sort who worked with his hands, so he contracted the services of a partnership of engineers, Bouton & Trepardoux, who were also brothers-in-law to each other.

Trepardoux privately offered the opinion that De Dion was a rich eccentric, whose ideas would be worthless. Bouton half agreed with this, but suggested to his brother-in-law that De Dion's money was just as good as anyone else's, and who knew? There just might be a little profit in it, above and beyond what De Dion was willing to pay. In any event, they had nothing to lose.

A steam automobile of 1884.
THE BETTMAN ARCHIVE, INC.

39

To Trepardoux's surprise, De Dion's ideas were a good deal more sound than he thought possible. More important, he was willing to advance the money for ideas the brothers-in-law had. One of these was for a very efficient, lightweight, quick-steam boiler invented by Bouton and built with De Dion's money. De Dion money also financed the development of a very practical, highly efficient, final-drive and rear-axle assembly, which the firm announced was a mutual effort of the Count de Dion and Monsieur Trepardoux.

There is reason to believe that De Dion's contribution to the axle was more in the order of writing checks than anything else, but the axle, still in use today on all sorts of automobiles from trucks to race cars, continues to bear his name.

During the next decade, Bouton & Trepardoux built all sorts of steam-powered vehicles. To Trepardoux's utter surprise, the Count not only began to make a little money on his investment, but also changed the status of Bouton & Trepardoux from employees to partners. The firm built everything from tricycles to trucks, and enough of the vehicles were successful so that Trepardoux was on the verge of admitting that he had been wrong about the Count all along.

At that point, De Dion made a surprising announcement for an aristocrat. The future of the automobile, he said, was in mass transportation, and since the mass could not afford to support a man or stoker (in French, a *chauffeur*), simply to keep the fire hot under the boiler, then the boiler had to go. The stinking gas engine, with all its attendant problems, was obviously the answer.

Monsieur Trepardoux threw up his hands in Gallic outrage. "I quit," he said, among a great many other things, and De Dion and Bouton bought him out. His decision to leave the partnership ranks high in the list of bad economic decisions; the partnership, and the gas engines that went with it, was to make Bouton richer than he could possibly have dreamed, and the Count even more "comfortable," as the aristocracy says.

Following Daimler's principles, and spending De Dion's money, Bouton went to work building his own engine. His first, completed in the fall of 1894, was a tiny (137 cubic centimeter displacement) one-lunger developing three-quarters of a horsepower. This was equivalent to 4 hp per liter[†]. Obviously that was not going to be powerful enough to propel the vehicles the partners had in mind. There were two ways they could increase the power. The first solution that came to mind was to make the engine larger. This looked like the only answer, for everyone except Bouton and De Dion agreed that it was practically impossible to improve on German technological know-how.

The second—impossible—solution, the one Bouton

[†]Europeans measure engine efficiency by use of the liter, which is slightly more than a quart in liquid measure and generally confusing to Americans, even today. The liter is defined as the volume occupied by 1 kilogram (1,000 grams, or 1.057 quarts) of pure water. 1.057 quarts of water also occupies 61.025 cubic inches. 1 liquid quart occupies exactly 57.75 cubic inches or 0.946 liter.

This steam carriage was built in England in 1862. CULVER

and De Dion decided they would use, was to increase the speed of the engine, despite much solemn and dire prophecy that 700–800 rpm was all that an engine could stand, no matter how well designed or well-constructed it was.

Within two years, by 1896, Bouton had designed and built an engine of 250 cc displacement which generated 1.75 hp, for the theoretical equivalent of 7 hp per liter.

He did this by building an engine with double the operating speed of the Daimler engine: 1,500 rpm. The Bouton engine was, moreover, capable of reaching 3,000 rpm for brief periods without tearing itself apart.

It was a major breakthrough, accomplished by beating the Germans at their own game. Great attention was paid to machining tolerances. Pistons and other moving parts were greatly reduced in weight, and matched, so that operating stresses would be reduced as much as possible.

De Dion and Bouton immediately began to make other engines, many of them far larger. There was a ready market for an engine twice as efficient as the Daimler and four times as efficient as the Benz.

Some engines, of course, were used as stationary engines. Others were used as the power for all sorts of vehicles from motorcycles (the word was just coming into use) to trucks. The larger engines had water-filled cooling jackets around the cylinders.

In 1899 De Dion-Bouton first marketed a *voiturette* (*voiture* is French for car; the addition of 'ette' implies a smaller version, as in kitchenette), powered by a three and a half horsepower water-cooled engine, a live (power-turned) rear axle and a constant-mesh, two-speed transmission. It was designed with De Dion's "mass transportation for the mass" principle in mind and was an immediate success.

Meanwhile, back in Germany:

In November of 1890, Gottleib Daimler emerged from his garden workshop and with suitable protocol and ceremony signed the articles of incorporation of Daimler Motoren G.m.b.H., an adequately financed entity with the intention of making motor cars for the public. It had a blue-ribbon board of directors and elaborate, well-thought-out plans to bring Germany into the motor age. The well-thought-out plans were set somewhat askew when Daimler promptly got in an argument with the blue-ribbon board of directors, and quit, again taking Herr Maybach with him.

An engineer named George Schrodter was thrown into his place, and told to make cars without their inventor and chief engineer on hand. What Schrodter built, and Daimler sold, were improved versions of the belt-driven carriage of 1889. They sold, increasing well (six hundred in 1899 alone) for the next decade, although they had a top speed of no more than 15 mph. They were reliable, and they were reasonably quiet.

Daimler and Maybach spent the next five years as consulting engineers. By then, it became apparent to the directors and stockholders of Daimler Motoren G.m.b.H. that if they were to catch up with the French, their best chance was by making peace with Gottlieb Daimler himself. In 1895, Daimler returned to the firm, towing Maybach along behind him.

The two moved slowly, improving what they'd already built, rather than starting fresh. The Daimler came out with a honeycomb radiator, and then a "gated"-gear selection system very much like a current stick shift. In 1899, some Daimlers were produced with a low-voltage ignition system developed by Simms-Bosch G.m.b.H. replacing the hot-platinum-tube ignition system.

The Bosch name today is to German—and other European—automobiles as Autolite or AC is to American cars.

In the same year, almost as if to show up the French, Daimler produced a radically new car. It had a 5.5 liter engine developing 24 hp and was capable of a really incredible 50 mph. The steering (not to mention such minor things as tires, suspension, and brakes) was not safe at that speed, of course, but then, as now, speed sells.

It was Daimler's swan song; he died shortly after the introduction of the car he called the Phoenix, a none-too-subtle reminder to the world in general that the Phoenix, the most powerful, the fastest, most elegant car in the world, had been built only after he and Maybach had, so to speak, been "called back from the ashes."

With Daimler gone, Maybach, fully aware that the world wasn't ready for a 50-mph automobile, revamped it so that it would go only 35-mph, but far more safely. There was also another problem. The largest potential market for the car was France and the French weren't particularly fond of the Germans. Daimler sounded far too German they said in that turn of the century market analysis, and something else was required.

Emile Jellinek, a Daimler salesman who finally became sales director, had a daughter with a name that wouldn't offend the French. Daimler's final *Phoenix* was put on sale as the first *Mercedes*.

With the exception of E. J. Pennington, the American influence on the automobile was hardly felt, if even noticed, in Europe at this time. E. J. Pennington was an admirer of Phineas T. Barnum, whose motto was "There's a sucker born every minute." Pennington went to England in 1896 with some highly imaginative designs for a highly improbable motorcycle. This machine, said Pennington, would go so fast that momentum alone would carry it across a sixty-foot-wide river.

He seemed like one of the brighter Americans and such an honest man, that the Lawson Automobile Syndicate paid him £100,000 (then the equivalent of about half a million dollars) for the rights to manufacture his machine. Shortly thereafter Pennington left the country, never to be seen there again. If there ever had been a working model of Pennington's machine, he must have taken it with him, for a rather extensive search of the British Isles failed to turn up a trace of it.

In 1927, a photographer named Walter Lewis went before a Notary Public, and gave a deposition to the effect that in 1891 he had taken a picture or pictures of a three-wheeled gas buggy invented by a man named Lambert.

Why he waited thirty-six years to make this pronouncement was never satisfactorily explained, and most historians agree that credit for making the first American automobile belongs to either, or both, of the Duryea brothers. They fought between themselves in their later years, each claiming the honor for himself.

It is a matter of official record that the Duryea Motor Waggon Company was founded in 1895, making it without question the first American automobile company.

Most cars in the United States were imported from Europe. The Steinway Company announces itself today to be piano manufacturers to the great artists of our time, but apparently around the turn of the century someone in their corporate heirarchy wasn't entirely sure that music was to be the company's future. Steinway Piano Company became in 1891 the American licensee of Herr Daimler's patents and imported a number of the German cars.

There were very few paved roads for cars and trucks. Laid end to end, all the paved roads in the United States at the turn of the century would have reached only between Boston and New York.

The Duryea horseless carriage really looked like a horseless carriage. The lever which served as the steering mechanism, looked very much like the wagon tongue bent

The Duryea horseless carriage of 1892-93, now in the U.S. National Museum in Washington, D.C. BROWN BROTHERS

backward. A one-cylinder engine was mounted over the rear wheels. But it ran, and it sold, and the Duryea brothers get the credit for the first automobile manufacturing business in the United States.

There is no doubt whatever that no matter who was first, the man who put America, and in a large measure, the world, on wheels was Henry Ford.

He was born on July 30, 1863, eight miles west of Detroit, Michigan, in a tiny little town known as Greenfield. His father, William, was English, although he had been born in Ireland. William Ford came to the United States as an immigrant in 1847. He apparently was not the archtypical impoverished immigrant who came to this country with nothing but hope and the clothing on his back, for he went immediately to Michigan and bought with cash, a forty-acre farm from a man named Litogot.

Fifteen years later, he married Farmer Litogot's daughter, Mary. When her parents died, William Ford inherited their farm, giving him a total of 240 acres. When his first son, Henry was born, he was a successful, fairly well-to-do farmer with a good reputation and greater prospects.

Father and Mother Ford were stocky people who loved their farm. Henry was tall and lanky, and he disliked mucking around in the dirt, although he thought that farming was a perfectly fine occupation for other people.

There is a story that at a very tender age he took his father's watch apart and saved himself a beating by getting it back together before Dad returned from the fields. The story is probably in the same category as George Washington's "I cannot tell a lie; I cut down the cherry tree," but it is true that as a very young man, he did work for a watchmaker named McGill in Detroit.

It is also true that in the Ford family barn, young Henry established his first workshop. There was a small forge, a vise, some hand tools, and a lathe driven by a bow. (The string of the bow was slack and wrapped around what was to be turned. Moving the bow back and forth turned the piece against the cutting tool.) It was enough, when Henry Ford was twelve or so, to earn him a reputation as a clever young man who could fix things.

He much preferred to fix things rather than walk behind the family plow. His preference did not sit well with his father. At sixteen he left home under unpleasant, but for the day, not uncommon, conditions. He was going to find his fortune in the city as a mechanic. So far as Father Ford was concerned, the city was no place for young men, especially his sons.

Against his father's wishes, Henry Ford went all the way to Detroit, eight miles distant. The United States had imported from England a custom which would today seem outrageous. If a young man wanted to learn a trade, he "apprenticed himself" to someone in the business. In exchange for long hours of his labor, the "craftsman" concerned would teach the apprentice the trade, feed him, house him, and once in a great while pay him a token wage. Henry Ford, aged sixteen, apprenticed himself to the Flowers Brothers Machine Shop of Detroit, a firm employing a total of twenty to forty apprentices, journeyman craftsmen, and master machinists, who were both in the business of building steam engines and of offering their skills and rudimentary machinery to the public at large.

Apparently the Flowers Brothers were for their day

either enlightened employers or very generous ones. Apprentice Ford had his nights and Sundays free, which was practically unheard of. It had double significance: First, Ford could thus spend his nights investigating the complexities of watches at McGill's; and second, it apparently gave him almost revolutionary ideas about the treatment of workers, ideas that he would later put into practice when he quite literally *was* the Ford Motor Company.

After nine months with Flowers Brothers, Henry Ford went to work for the Dry Dock Engine Company, the largest machine shop in Detroit, whose almost sole occupation was of building steam engines for service on Lake Michigan steamers.

While the proprietors of the Dry Dock Engine Company were willing to admit after two years that nineteen-year-old Henry Ford was one of their brighter apprentices, they were not quite willing to go along with Ford's announcement that, so far as he was concerned, he was a master machinist and should be paid as such. They parted company.

Ford was able to convince John Cheeny, the state agent for Westinghouse Steam Engines, that he was a master machinist. Cheeny hired him, and put him to work as his "road expert," a somewhat misleading title intended to convey that young Ford would go on the road as an expert, rather than being an expert about roads.

Westinghouse at that time was selling two basic models of stationary steam engines, developing 10 hp and 20 hp. Ford's job was to accompany new engines to their destinations, set them up, and instruct their new owners in their use and maintenance. He would also visit owners when the machines broke down and needed repairs.

It was a warm-weather, or summertime job, and in the winters Cheeny gave Ford work in his own small machine shop. For two winters Ford built, experimented with, and improved a steam tractor.

There seems to be no question whatever that by the time Henry Ford was twenty-one, he was not only a first class mechanical, as they were then called, but the master machinist he announced himself to be. He was also something of an expert about steam engines, both stationary ones and those used for vehicle propulsion.

William Ford, however, was unimpressed with his son's accomplishments. No matter how well Henry had done, he could, and should, do better as a gentleman farmer. Father Ford was in a position to entice his eldest son back to the soil. He bought forty acres of timber land for Henry. It was so valuable a piece of property, and so genuine a gesture of reconciliation, that Ford simply couldn't refuse.

The Buckeye Harvester Company, which built portable steam engines for use on farm equipment, were delighted to have Henry Ford make himself available to repair their malfunctioning steam engines during the summer. He had a reputation for being a hard worker and being absolutely reliable. He also neither chewed tobacco nor had any interest in liquor, two character traits rather rare amongst farm machinery repairmen.

He rented a twelve horsepower steam engine to drive a sawmill and went into the lumber business in the winter when the steam engine repair business of the summer months fell off. Like just about everything else he did in his life, his various jobs both gave him an astonishing fund of knowledge which he was able to put to use when he went into the automobile business and also made him money.

When he was twenty-four, he married a neighbor, Clara J. Bryant. His father, after watching Henry's two years of successful operation as a lumber manufacturer and part-time steam engine repairer, was just about convinced that Henry was coming to his senses. With the lumber chopped down, what else was there to do with forty acres but farm? Any man with land would certainly be smart enough to farm it.

Henry Ford, however, announced that he was going to build a horseless carriage, putting to work his experience as a steam-engine expert.

He took a standard carriage and fitted it with a steam engine. The carriage had a sixty-inch wheelbase, and there were fifty-six inches between the wheels, making it very nearly square.

The transmission and steam engine itself proved little of a problem for a man experienced in powering machinery with steam engines. He built a single-cylinder engine, "square" with a two inch piston moving through a two-inch stroke. Power moved, after passing through double-reduction gears, via a belt from the crankshaft to a sprocket shaft. It was transferred by a chain drive from the first sprocket to the differential-gear sprocket, and then to the divided axles which turned the wheels. It was neat, workmanlike, and reliable.

The boiler, however, posed to Henry Ford the same problems that it had to every experimenter with mobile steam boilers since Serpollet. It worked, but not well.

Ford was a determined man, and after he had built Ford versions of the common types of boilers—water tube, fire tube, and flash, or instantaneous designs—he built them again, this time taking pains unusual even for a craftsman like Ford.

It was his first failure. He could not manufacture a satisfactory mobile steam boiler, no matter which principle he followed, no matter with what care and precision the boiler was constructed.

Steam, he announced to his father, was obviously not the answer to a satisfactory power plant for the horseless carriage. This did not mean that he was either abandoning the idea of a horseless carriage, or that he was going to settle down on his forty acres and devote himself to making a decent living from the soil.

Not that he had anything against earning a decent living. Nor was he troubled with false modesty. The large and growing Detroit Edison Illuminating Company (now simply, Detroit Edison) was in need of a night-shift engineer at their generating plant. This was the sort of job that went to men who had spent their careers with the company, men in their late fifties and early sixties. It was not the sort of a job given to twenty-five-year-olds.

Ford applied for the job, got it, and rented out the Dearborn farm. He took his wife to Detroit, rented a house at 58 Bagley Street, two blocks from the plant, and went to work for $45 a month. His hours were from six at night to six in the morning, seven days a week.

He later said that he took the job to have time to work on his horseless carriage. He first built a small barn at the rear of the Bagley Street property (the word "barn" is somewhat misleading; it was a small brick structure, about twenty feet by ten) and then moved his tools from the farm into it.

While he had no intention of spending the rest of his life generating electricity for Detroit Edison and could not be said to have really tried to impress his superiors, he was congenitally unable to be anything but what he was: a first class mechanic, a master machinist, and a hard-working, highly intelligent young man. Three months after going to work for Detroit Edison, his pay was raised to $75 a month, a large amount of money in those days, and after he had been there nine months, he was named chief engineer of the main generating plant at $100 a month. To commemorate his first year of employment, he was raised to $125.

It would have taken action by the Board of Directors to increase his salary above $125. That was a vast sum, far more than a young man in his twenties had any right to expect, far more than a man with only a wife to support could reasonably spend.

Henry Ford (third from right, top row) shortly after joining Detroit Edison.

DETROIT EDISON

Henry Ford (third from left) at the Washington Boulevard power plant of Detroit Edison.

DETROIT EDISON

For the seven years that Henry Ford was the chief engineer of the main generating plant of Detroit Edison, his pay was not raised. For it, he was expected to be present at the plant, either in person, or available on a moment's notice, twenty-four hours a day, seven days a week.

This didn't pose much of a problem for him, for he was spending all of his spare time in the "barn" behind the house on Bagley Street, building his first internal-combustion engine, and then along with it, the first gasoline-powered Ford automobile.

On Christmas Eve, 1893, Clara Ford was told to leave the turkey in the oven—her husband had need of her. She

Henry Ford's February 25, 1896 payroll at Detroit Edison. DETROIT EDISON

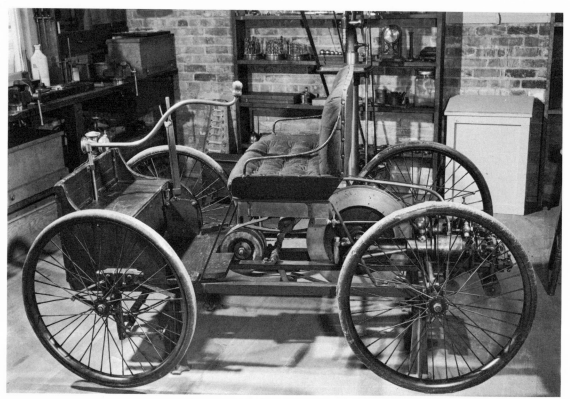

The 1896 quadricycle—Henry Ford's first car. FORD ARCHIVES

went out to the brick building and saw the first Ford
gasoline engine. It looked like a stationary engine, and
compared to the huge steam engines her husband was re-
sponsibile for, it wasn't at all impressive. It had a round
base about four inches in diameter, supporting about four
inches above it the cylinder, which was about a foot long.
The base supported the piston in such a manner that it
looked something like a cannon.

58

The piston rod (coming out of the "barrel" of the cannon) was exposed and much longer than the cylinder, and turned a small crankshaft some eighteen or twenty inches from the end of the cylinder.

Henry Ford handed his wife a container of gasoline and a wad of cotton. He showed her where to hold the cotton (over the intake manifold of the engine) and how rapidly she was to drip gasoline onto the wadding. Then, for ignition, he plugged into the main line of the house, getting his electricity from the generators of Detroit Edison. The engine had a simple make-and-break mechanism to deliver a spark to the combustion chamber at the proper time. Mrs. Ford dripped the gasoline, Henry Ford turned the shaft, and with something less than a mighty roar, the first Ford engine came to life.

It worked. Henry Ford would have been surprised if it had not done so. He built it for the experience, to see and feel for himself how pieces of machined steel could be put into motion by the forces generated by burning gasoline vapor. The first engine obviously wasn't powerful enough to power a car, so, once built, it was run briefly, and then put aside.

(But not very far aside: As late as 1914, when Ford was already a millionaire many times over and had made more automobiles than everybody else in the world put together, that first engine could be found sitting on the drawing board in the private office of Edsel Bryant Ford, next door to Henry Ford.)

Satisfied now that the internal-combustion engine was

*This photograph of Henry Ford,
seated in his first automobile, was
taken in 1896, when Ford was
thirty-three years old.*

FORD ARCHIVES

the answer to what he was already thinking of as the Fordmobile, Ford began to build his first car.

It was not really very much different from the cars built by other men in Europe and America. It had a horizontal, two-cylinder, water-cooled engine, moving 2 $\frac{9}{16}$-inch pistons through a 6-inch stroke. He used 28-inch bicycle wheels, with a 42-inch gauge (from side to side) and a 60-inch wheelbase. There was an open-top water reservoir, but no water pump; water circulated because of the difference in temperatures.

There seems to be a good deal of disagreement as to when it was first driven over the roads of Detroit. In his autobiography, Henry Ford ties its first appearance to the annual return to Detroit of a small bird called the bobolink. He said he was "running it when the bobolinks came." In other words, according to Ford, in the spring of 1893.

According to the Automobile Manufacturer's Association, however, Mr. Ford's memory was off by three years and two months. They say that the first Ford ran in Detroit on June 4, 1896.

Precisely when Henry Ford built his car isn't really as important as the fact that not only did he build one car, and then another, but he went on to build a dozen, and a hundred, and ultimately millions, while his contemporaries in the new business of building cars built just one, or two, or perhaps fifty at the most.

CHAPTER V The Chambers of Commerce in Allentown and Bethlehem, adjacent communities in eastern Pennsylvania, state flatly that one Henry Nadig ran a gasoline-powered vehicle over their streets in 1891. They even have a picture of Mr. Nadig's car.

History may go back even beyond that. A man named Olds, assisted by his twenty-one-year-old son, Ransom E. Olds, built a satisfactory gas engine in 1885. At the same time, another gas engine was developed and built by H. K. Shanks, who proudly showed it off at the Ohio State Fair of 1886. One of the spectators who was fascinated by the engine was Charles Duryea. He not only decided he was going to build his own car, but talked his brother Frank into helping him.

That the Brothers Duryea built a car is beyond question. The car itself is now in the Smithsonian Institution. They generally are credited with doing so years before Henry Ford did, but even here there's disagreement. Charles Duryea said that he first drove the car he designed on April 19, 1892. Not so, said Brother Frank: "I drove it first, and the date was September 20, 1893."

Way back in 1876, an attorney, George B. Selden, who was a sort of frustrated engineer, built a gasoline engine that ran. He realized that he was on to a good thing, and in 1879, applied for a patent for a gasoline-engine-propelled vehicle.

He never actually built the car he patented. What he did was to submit to the patent office a drawing of a self-propelled vehicle, with letters identifying the various

Frank Duryea in the car that won the Thanksgiving Day race, 1895. BROWN BROTHERS

parts, wheels, body, motor, steering tiller, and so forth. (It would have been very much the same if Robert Goddard, the rocket expert who predicted space flight, had submitted a drawing to the patent office with letters identifying the various parts of the rocket (head, body, and rocket engine) and had been granted a patent without anyone questioning how the rocket engine worked, or how the passengers were to be kept alive.)

Selden got his patent, and then vanished, to pop up later and cause all sorts of interesting problems for the automobile business.

After proving that he could build a horseless carriage, Frank Duryea set about building a better one. His second car was a considerable improvement over the first, which had been nothing more than a powered, third-hand buggy. The new car had wooden wheels, solid rubber tires, and its machinery was neatly enclosed. It had a water-cooled engine, three forward speeds and reverse, and turned a wholly satisfactory 18 mph.

About the time he had finished his second car, the newspapers were carrying the story of the incredible Paris-Rouen automobile race in France. Automobile racing, decided a Chicago newspaper, might be just the thing to boost circulation, so, in the interests of scientific advancement and national pride, the *Times-Herald* came up with a $5,000 Purse for a Thanksgiving Day 1895 Race from Chicago to Evanston and return.

There were ninety-five entrants, but when race time came, only six cars showed up: three German Benz, two electric-battery cars, and the Duryea. One of the Benz cars had been entered by R. H. Macy, the New York City merchant. Frank Duryea ran away with the race, covering the distance at a mind-staggering 6.66 mph.

The race proved two things in the minds of many people. First, that an American car was capable of being just as reliable as, and much faster, than any European car, and second, that gasoline engines were obviously the answer to the problem of power.

Meanwhile, a dignified, rather portly gentleman named Ellwood Haynes was employed as a field superintendent for a natural gas company in Kokomo, Indiana. He had some experience with gas, both natural, and that by-product of oil refining, "gasoilene," and he had a certain degree of practical engineering knowledge. Enough, in

The Haynes-Apperson Gasoilene Buggy, built in Kokomo, Indiana and demonstrated successfully on July 4, 1894. BROWN BROTHERS

other words, to design a car. Equally important, he also had enough money to indulge his fancy.

He took the design to a machine shop run by two brothers, Edgar and Elmer Apperson. They had long said they could build anything out of metal, and they accepted Haynes' challenge with a good bit of confidence. Long before the car was near completion, they announced, that they would demonstrate it on Independence Day, 1894.

On the Fourth of July, to the considerable surprise of just about everyone but Haynes and the Apperson Brothers, the Haynes-Apperson Gasoilene Buggy ran as scheduled, at the magnificent speed of better than six miles per hour.

It was Mr. Haynes intention to enter the *Times-Herald* race, but he collided with a street car en route to the starting point, leaving unanswered for all time the question of what would have happened had there been two American Gas Buggies in the great Chicago-Evanston race.

Haynes and the Apperson Brothers formed the Haynes-Apperson Company in 1895, for the express purpose of building and selling automobiles. The Duryea Brothers formed the Duryea Motor Waggon Company about this time, and made their first sale, in February 1896 to George H. Morrill, Jr., of Norwood, Massachusetts. This generally is considered to be the first commercial sale of an automobile in the United States.

On March 6, 1896, Charles B. King, according to the

Detroit *Free Press,* drove "the first horseless carriage seen in this city . . . last night." Since Henry Ford had announced that he had driven the first car in Detroit several years before, it isn't really surprising that no mention is made in his autobiography of the story that made the rounds at the time that the chief engineer of the Detroit Edison Illuminating Company, wearing a bowler, was seen chasing the horseless carriage on his bicycle.

All the evidence seems to suggest that Mr. Ford's memory was faulty about when the first Ford actually appeared, because in most other respects the details in the story of the developing automobile are the same in both Ford's and other people's versions. There is no record, in any Detroit newspaper of either date of the first road trip of the first Ford.

On the other hand, there is a good deal of evidence that Ford not only knew Charles B. King, but that he borrowed tools from him, and sought his engineering advice, although he didn't necessarily agree with the advice he was given, or follow it to any significant degree.

Ford had the idea that the lighter a car was the better. He put this into practice with his first car, which weighed five hundred pounds. King's car was nearly three times heavier, thirteen hundred pounds. The Haynes-Apperson weighed over eight hundred, and the Duryea about seven hundred.

Henry Ford's father was still not very impressed. He refused to ride in the "quadricycle" (as Ford called it, doubling the two wheel bicycle), saying that he could see no good reason to risk his life. Mrs. Ford had more faith in her husband; the first trip in the car was to carry her and baby Edsel out in the country to see the folks.

The first Ford was sold for $200, and the money used to build a third car. In the meantime, Ford had decided that the way to make money with automobiles was to make as many of them as possible. He set out to find money. It was difficult. It took him three years to get enough money to start the Detroit Automobile Company, organized with $15,000. He was then faced with another choice. The Detroit Edison Company was aware that automobiles had become more than a pastime for him. They told him they were going to promote him to General Superintendent, with one condition: that he give up the automobile, and devote himself to the affairs of the company.

On August 15, 1899, he quit.

His new job, as production superintendent of the Detroit Automobile Company, paid him less money than he'd been earning, although he did have a small block of stock. What really bothered him was an almost total lack of authority. The direction of the company, the backers politely but firmly informed him, was none of his affair. The company adopted a practice of first selling a car, and then building it. Henry Ford's contribution was to oversee the construction of one car at a time, one after the other, in a manner very much like a building construction superintendent of the present day. The parallel went further. The car was sold for what the buyer was willing to pay, as houses often are, rather than with regard to cost of manufacture. And finally, they were built like houses. In one place, with one part after another added by hand, until the whole car was completed.

In a year, the Detroit Automobile Company produced twenty cars, and was then dissolved. Henry Ford was without a job, but it can't really be said that he was broke and desperate. It seems that he was perfectly content when Detroit Automobile folded; it struck him as a dead-end street.

He'd noticed that the greatest interest of the American people was in speed, rather than any other characteristic of the automobile. Ford decided he would have to cater to their whim, although he thought that a race car made about as much sense as a six-legged horse.

His first race car carried a two-cylinder engine, developing an entirely respectable twenty-six horsepower. This wasn't half as powerful as the car Ford challenged, a 70-hp monster built by Alexander Winton, a car which had already proven its ability by covering a measured mile in 1:14.5, or a dizzying 48-mph plus.

In October, 1901, Ford met Winton at the Grosse Pointe race track, for a ten mile race. Winton's car dashed ahead for an early lead, and kept gaining on Henry Ford. And then Winton's car came apart. Ford passed him, and won the race, announcing when it was over that it had been his first and last appearance on the race course. Winton was the better driver, Ford announced, and if he were at the tiller of the Ford, he would beat anything on wheels.

The 1901 Ford quadricycle with a steering tiller. FORD ARCHIVES

Henry Ford, with Barney Oldfield at the wheel of the "999."
FORD MOTOR COMPANY

Alexander Winton driving his first automobile. BROWN BROTHERS

He'd guessed right about what people really wanted to see in a car. They wanted speed, they wanted a winning car. Some of the people who had backed Detroit Automobile now came forth again with their checkbooks, and the Henry Ford Company was formed. They wanted his name as a winning racer and they wanted his proven expertise as a machinist, but they still didn't think he had what it took to be a successful businessman. He was again in charge of production, and this time he had about one-sixth of the stock in the company.

Ford immediately began to have differences with his associates. He wanted to spend time, money, and effort building race cars, not because he was so fond of racing, but because it had been proved to his complete satisfaction that racing was the best possible advertisement for a car.

Perversely, the same people who backed him in the second venture were the ones who had agreed with his arguments in the now defunct Detroit Automobile Company. They wanted to make cars and have them available for sale to all comers, rather than to "custom" build them. And now Ford, who had said he agreed with this, wanted to waste time and good money racing.

Ford was not very malleable. To get him to change his position would require a man of even stronger will, and a firm belief that he was right and everybody else was wrong. The Henry Ford Company's Board of Directors appointed one Henry M. Leland as "advisor" to the budding company. He was a man of great dignity, many years older than Ford, and the power behind Faulconer

& Leland—the best and the largest machine shop in the United States.

Their differences can be summed up simply and reasonably accurately by saying that Leland believed first, that an article's price, whatever the article, was as much as the seller could get for it, and second, that the manufacture of anything metallic, including automobiles, should start by first designing it with great care, and then building it from blueprints. Henry Ford had nothing against blueprints, but at this stage of automobile development he thought it made a great deal more sense to make the part work, and then measure it, so blueprints of it could be made, rather than the other way around, which took far too much time.

In March, 1902, Henry Ford parted company with the Henry Ford Company. As part of the price of getting rid of him, he insisted that the company not be allowed to market cars with his name on them. In other words, the Henry Ford Company could not sell Fords.

Henry immediately announced that he was going to build even better racers, and started construction of two cars, "999" and "The Arrow." They would be known, of course, as the "Ford 999" and the "Ford Arrow" which put the Henry Ford Company in a somewhat awkward position. The company was reorganized, and a new name chosen: "The Cadillac Automobile Company."

A major race was scheduled for October, 1902, at the same Grosse Pointe, Michigan, track where Henry Ford had run his first and only race. They hired a bicycle racer named Barney Oldfield to drive the 999. It was a

One of the first gasoline cars sold by Olds, in 1897. BROWN BROTHERS

huge beast of a car, even by today's standards. There were almost five and a half feet between the wheels for tread, and the wheelbase was 117 inches. Four seven-inch diameter pistons moved through a seven-inch stroke developing 70 hp, as much as the Winton car. It had the tiller-lever steering mechanism, but it was so large and heavy that two handles were fitted to the tiller at right angles.

Oldfield won the race hands down, easily defeating Winton's racer, and other cars as well.

Ford had been right. The success of his racer meant that he could now get money to build what his detractors called a "family horse." In 1903, the fourth attempt to start a company resulted in the Ford Motor Company, and this time, there was incredible success. But he was starting late.

Ransom Eli Olds, the young man whose father's engine had been shown at the 1885 Ohio State Fair, had matured into a first class mechanic and businessman whose skill had put him successfully into the automobile business. Olds sold his first gasoline car in 1896. He got financing from S. L. Smith, who had made his millions in copper, and who advanced the money on the condition that his two sons be given jobs. By 1899, Olds was in production. He started out with an elegant machine, which had, among other things, an electric push-button starter, and which sold for $1,250. It was not a success; the company lost $80,000 in their first year of operation.

Olds discarded the whole idea, and came up with a car that was quite simple. It had an enclosed, rear-mounted

This horseless carriage was designed and built by Ransom Eli Olds in 1886-87.

BROWN BROTHERS

The Stanley brothers in their steam car. BROWN BROTHERS

One of the first police cars in America was this 1900 Stanley Steamer, used by the Boston police force. BROWN BROTHERS

The 1914 Stanley Steamer touring car. This car was restored by an antique auto hobbyist. NATIONAL ARCHIVES

engine, a single seat big enough to hold three thin people or two heavy ones; a tiller lever, and a curved dash. There were mudguards at dashing angles over front and rear wheels, and two brass lanterns—the first headlights.

It was a success because it was far cheaper than the other car, and also, it has been suggested, because its simple functional design had an appeal all of its own. In 1901, more than four hundred "Oldsmobiles" had been sold, and by 1905, production was more than sixty-five hundred.

And, of course, an enterprising tunesmith had recognized a good thing when he saw it, and composed a popular song about the car: "In My Merry Oldsmobile." That was a delightful free advertisement, and just might well be considered the first singing commercial.

In Kenosha, Wisconsin, in 1902 Thomas B. Jeffery had started production of a car called the "Rambler," and he was doing rather well with it when the Ford Motor Company came into being.

Among other new entries into the automobile business were cars powered by electricity and steam. Both had theoretical advantages over the gasoline car, as well as some practical advantages. What had happened in Europe reoccurred here. Electric cars were built, tested, and advertised. They proved quiet, simple, reliable, and cheap to operate, and then died because their range was only twenty or twenty-five miles.

Steam cars had the same sort of history. The most notable of these were built by the brothers Stanley, identical twins called by their initials, F.O. and F.E. The first successful Stanley Steamer was put on the road in 1897. It had an appeal to the public that even Henry Ford and the 999 could not later match. It was said, with truth, that no one had ever dared drive a Stanley Steamer as fast as it would go. On the beach at Daytona, Florida (which remained a car testing ground until 1959), a Stanley Steamer racer, called a Wogglebug, did the measured mile in 28.2 seconds, which is a little better than 125 mph.

But steam required large quantities of water, which took up too much space and weighed too much for real success. Although Steamers lasted until the 1920's, they didn't really offer much competition to the gas burners.

(They're far from dead, however, and neither are the electrics, as we shall see in later chapters.)

Using the word loosely, there were three thousand or more "manufacturers," during the period 1900–1908. Some of these were quite bona fide. The bulk, however, consisted of two or three people who got together, bought themselves an engine, a carriage, and some gearing, and announced they were in business. They said that all it would take to make everyone rich would be a small investment by their forward-looking friends and relatives.

Those who could be considered to be more interested in making automobiles than a fast buck, in other words, those who really wanted to go into business and who made genuine efforts to get a factory, and a sales organization underway, numbered around five hundred. At least that many serious automobile companies were started, in any event, during the period 1900–1908; more than three hundred failed in the same period.

CHAPTER VI The years at the turn of the century were some of the most exciting years in the history of the country. The United States, in 1898, thought of itself as what we would today call an "emerging" country. We weren't exactly ashamed of ourselves, but we still looked to Europe for an example to follow.

In those days, Brittania really did rule the waves, and was the most industrialized country in the world, closely followed by Germany. (Karl Marx, who had lived in Germany and England and the United States, visualized his communism, or state ownership of the means of production, for Germany and England rather than for Russia, which was then about as industrially backward comparatively as it is now.)

We were, in the 1890's, still having our trouble with the Indians. We'd only had a transcontinental railroad since 1869, and vast areas of the country were still wilderness.

The Spanish-American War, and the President who came out of it, Theodore Roosevelt, changed this. The American Giant was already stirring in its sleep when the battleship, *Maine*, blew up and sank in Havana harbor. Cuba was then a Spanish colony. Egged on by newspapers, America went to war with great enthusiasm. Whatever resentment still remained between the North and South because of the Civil War seemed to be wiped out when Yankee and Rebel congressmen linked arms in the House of Representatives and sang "The Battle Hymn of the Republic" after they had declared war on Spain.

80

The first battle was at sea, off the coast of Cuba. The U. S. Navy won hands down. American troops landed at Santiago, stormed up Kettle and San Juan Hill, and defeated the Spanish Army. Across the world, the United States Navy, without losing a man, sank the Spanish Asiatic Fleet at the Battle of Manila Bay. Spain sued for peace.

The former British colony had taken on a major European power and with a remarkable lack of effort brought it quickly to its knees. Roosevelt, who came out of the war a colonel was swept into the presidency. As a practical demonstration of his new foreign policy, "Walk Softly and Carry A Big Stick," he had the Navy's battleships painted white and sent them on a long, around-the-world cruise.

This all took place at the time the automobile was changing from a fascinating toy into something real.

In Warren, Ohio, there was a man named James Ward Packard, who owned a successful business making electrical cables. In 1899, Packard bought a Winton, drove it around awhile, and then, with typical American bluntness, wrote a letter to Alexander Winton telling him he had bought one of his cars, and that it "was no good. I can—and will—make a better one myself."

He formed the Ohio Automobile Company and began to build Packards in his home town. One of them was parked outside the Automobile Show in New York City in 1901 where Henry Joy, of Detroit saw it. At the time Mr. Joy was a little discouraged with automobiles gen-

The first Packard, built in 1899. BROWN BROTHERS

erally, and steam cars specifically. The day before he saw the Packard, a steam car he'd been thinking of buying had blown up in his face, giving him an unwelcome shower and an unpleasant thrill. As he was looking at the Packard, its chauffeur arrived, gave the crank a spin, the engine caught, and away he drove.

Joy went to Warren, Ohio, and bought out the Packard Motor Company, taking it, and Mr. Packard, with him to Detroit. Packard kept his electric cable business. The Packard Motor Company began to produce a car costing nearly $8,000, and within a matter of years, had lost $200,000. Packard decided that the whole idea was a failure, and went back to making electrical cable.

The Packard company went on to make cars without Mr. Packard; eventually the Packard was the finest car made in America, and the firm continued in production until long after World War II. The PT boat which Lieutenant John F. Kennedy commanded in World War II was powered with Packard engines.

James Packard was not left out in the cold. Ultimately, he was able to sell his Packard Cable Company, very much in business today, to the General Motors Corporation for many millions.

In 1900, David Dunbar Buick was a successful and fairly well-to-do man. He and a partner had invented a technique to bake porcelain onto metal for bathtubs and other bathroom fixtures. (Before Buick's innovation, bathtubs and the like were either of sheet metal, which was ugly and rust-prone, or simply ceramic, like outsized

John (left) and Horace Dodge.
DODGE MOTOR COMPANY

83

water pitchers, which was expensive and fragile.) The money started to roll in, and David Dunbar Buick began to spend it just about as fast experimenting with the automobile.

His production left something to be desired. In 1903, Buick produced a total of sixteen cars. He barely doubled this in 1904, making thirty-seven Buicks.

The Buick Motor Company was then sold to a man named William Crapo Durant, who is more or less forgotten now, but who had as much to do with putting America on wheels—and, for cooling America's food— as anyone else.

He was the first of that particularly American phenomenon, the wheeler-dealer. He came from a solid background, and first went to work for his grandfather, in the lumber business. That wasn't nearly exciting enough for him, so he went into the insurance business. Before he was twenty-one, and legally able to sign an insurance policy, he had established the William C. Durant Insurance Agency, and he was well-off in his own right, without Grandpa's money or well-meaning advice.

Somewhere in the wilds of Michigan, running down a prospect for life insurance, Durant saw a horse-cart with a design that struck him as being clever, sound, and most important, saleable. He bought the design rights to it for the grand sum of fifty dollars, then spent several hundred dollars getting a patent for it.

He went into partnership with Dallas Dort, a clerk, whose duty it became to handle the administration while

David Buick. GENERAL MOTORS

Durant went out to make money. He placed an order—the largest horse-cart order ever given—for ten thousand wagons, paying a Flint, Michigan carriage maker $8.50 each. He had no trouble selling them for over twelve dollars. He made a small fortune with the horse-cart, then went into business with the Durant-Dort Carriage Company, manufacturing and selling carriages. In 1904, he was worth over a million dollars.

In that year, he bought the Buick Motor Company for about $75,000. That figure, while impressive, didn't seem to have the sound to it that William C. Durant thought necessary. By shuffling figures here and there, and by issuing extra certificates of stock (no cash changed hands) almost immediately he raised the capitalization (the theoretical worth) of the Buick Motor Company to $300,000.

William C. Durant. GENERAL MOTORS

That sounded a little more substantial, thought Mr. Durant, but it didn't sound as good as $500,000 would. Or, even better, $1,500,000.

Before the company could make the announcement that they were capitalized at one million, five-hundred thousand dollars, it was necessary to convince the government of the State of Michigan that either they had that much money, or assets worth that much, such as buildings, stocks of cars, parts, tools, and so on. Even by the most generous estimate of the value of Buick assets (some said an outright dishonest estimate) they were still some $60,000 short of the 1.5 million-dollar figure.

Durant had a quick solution to this. He announced that the company possessed plans for a new internal-combustion engine, so revolutionary that they didn't want to risk having it patented, and which they valued, by coincidence, at $60,000.

The State of Michigan, in all legal solemnity, certified that the Buick Motor Company had cash and assets, including the highly imaginary engine, worth $1,500,000.

It may not have been ethical or even honest, but it established the Buick Motor Company. Shortly thereafter, Mr. Buick left the company. Durant was on his way to forming General Motors.

Meanwhile Ransom Eli Olds was making Oldsmobiles for the Olds Motor Works, which is quite different from saying that he was making them for himself. There were twenty thousand shares of stock in the Olds Motor Works, and more than nineteen thousand of them were held by the copper man, S. L. Smith. Smith's sons, whose employment had been part of, and probably the reason for the deal by which Smith gave Olds the money, were now feeling their oats. They thought that the Oldsmobile should be larger, more luxurious, and more expensive than the current model. It should resemble, for example, a Daimler or a Benz.

They were used to having money, and getting their own way, and they didn't particularly care what Olds had to say about the mass production of cheap cars. When he threatened to quit over the issue, they quickly accepted his resignation, and Olds left Oldsmobile. Olds was right, of course, and the production of expensive Oldsmobiles steadily declined.

86

He himself went to Lansing, Michigan, and founded the Reo company, using his initials. The Reo Company made cars, and are still manufacturing heavy, quality, special application trucks.

Oldsmobile became the next horseless carriage in the stable of William C. Durant, in what was the embryonic General Motors Company.

Before Henry Ford had lost the respect of the solid citizens of Detroit by giving up his excellent, well-paid, and prestigious position as engineer for the Detroit Edison Illuminating Company in favor of the stinking horseless carriage, he made the acquaintance of Alexander T. Malcolmson. Mr. Ford had been buying coal, and Mr. Malcolmson, who had parlayed a one-horse wagon and some coal on credit into the largest coal business in Detroit, had been selling it.

Malcolmson was a man of some imagination, daring, and money. He didn't think Henry Ford was nearly as funny as most other people did. He thought it entirely possible that Henry might have the right solution to making money from the gasoline buggy.

The partnership of Malcolmson & Ford was formed, Malcolmson putting up $500, and Henry Ford putting up himself and his ideas. James Couzens, a Malcolmson employee, was hired to run things, and a man named Harold Wills, a friend and associate of Ford's, was put on the payroll at $125 a month.

The mechanical equipment of the first Ford Company consisted of a grinding wheel, a saw, some hand tools, a standard, foot-bellows blacksmith's forge, and two drill presses and lathes. The first factory, hardly larger than the building behind the Ford home of Bagley Street, was soon replaced by a converted wagon shop. It had been lying unused, and the owner agreed to refurnish it, providing that Malcolmson & Ford agreed to lease it for three years at seventy-five dollars a month.

That first Ford was assembled in December, 1902. It had a steering wheel (on the right) with controls for throttle (accelerator) and ignition on the steering wheel column. Electric power for the spark came from a double set of six dry-cell batteries. It had a Ford-designed planetary transmission, providing two speeds forward and one reverse. It was put on the market for $850 with a tonneau, $750 without it.

The car looked as though it would sell, but there was a problem. The partnership was fresh out of money to buy more parts to make more cars.

Mr. Ford was not the only Detroit eccentric of Malcolmson's acquaintance. He knew a pair of Irishmen—brothers—who rather astonished the more straitlaced citizenry of the community with their success at the machinist trade. They operated a machine shop that was second only to Faulconer & Leland in size and efficiency —some said it was even better—despite a certain proclivity for both the bottle and the brawl.

Horace and John Dodge, known then as "the Dodge Boys," had the habit of relaxing from the week's labor by visiting the less elegant saloons of Detroit on a Saturday night to see if they couldn't find a fight. They generally succeeded.

In personality, they were almost exactly the opposite of Henry Ford who never touched a drop, but professionally they understood each other. The first contract Malcolmson arranged with them provided for the Dodge Brothers to deliver more than six hundred chassis (frames, axles, engines, and transmissions) at a price of $250. Even perfectionist Henry Ford couldn't find fault with the Dodge Brothers' chassis, and the relationship lasted for more than eleven years, until the Dodge Brothers decided to go into the business of selling complete automobiles themselves.

Malcolmson let other contracts too. The Hartford Rubber Company would supply five tires for about $40; a carriage company agreed to build and supply the bodies and cushions for $68; there were others. Ford was really more an assembler of parts than a car manufacturer, despite the nameplate on the car.

Despite Malcolmson's financial position, however, and his willingness to put all of his resources into the new company, the expenses soon drained his bank account, and new sources of money had to be found almost immediately. Fortunately, Malcolmson had an indulgent uncle, John S. Gray, who was a banker.

Gray agreed to put up $10,500 immediately to pay money due the Dodge Brothers (who had announced that if the Ford Motor Company didn't instantly pay them, there would be no chassis) on the condition that the firm be incorporated, and that he be given 10.5 per cent of the stock.

Malcolmson and his friend and employee Couzens had been looking for money elsewhere, and for a time they thought they had found it in the person of Charles H. Bennett, a major stockholder in the profitable Daisy Air Rifle Company, the BB-gun manufacturer. The prototype Ford was shown to Bennett and he was instantly enthusiastic about both it and the prospects of the Ford Motor Company. The Daisy Air Rifle Company, he announced, would put up half the capital required to incorporate the Ford Motor Company.

The other stockholders of the Daisy Air Rifle Company were somewhat less enthusiastic than Mr. Bennett, and found a legal technicality in their articles of incorporation which forbade such an investment. Bennett's enthusiasm was undimmed, however, and when the incorporation actually took place, on June 16, 1903, he put in $5,000 of his own money.

One thousand shares of stock, with a par value of $100, were issued. Ford and Malcolmson were given 255 shares each, so that together with 510 shares, or 51 per cent of the whole, they had control of the company. Malcolmson's uncle received his promised 10 per cent, or 105 shares. For $7,000 worth of materials and an IOU for $3,000 the Dodge Brothers got one hundred shares. Other investors, including the carpenter who had converted the wagon shop to be the first Ford plant, lawyers, relatives, and friends, contributed either cash, or IOU's, so the entire one thousand shares were subscribed. There was $28,000 cash in the bank when all was over. One hundred dollars of this had belonged to James Couzens' sister, a school teacher, who had wagered half her life's savings. When she finally sold her one share of stock (par value $100) in 1916, she was paid $355,000 for it.

At the first director's meeting, it was agreed that Henry Ford and James Couzens should receive a salary. Ford was paid $300 a month and Couzens just over $200.

In the early part of July, 1903, the first Ford chassis arrived at the Ford plant, sent over from the Dodge Brothers Machine Works on horse-drawn wagons. They were carried by hand into the factory by the few workmen who were going to build that particular Ford, and set up on wooden horses. The small teams of men assembled them part by part. The wheels were put on, and the body, and the fenders. The car was painted by hand with brushes, and then, when it was dry, the whole car was picked bodily off the floor, the wooden sawhorses were removed, and the car was pushed outside for a run-up and test drive.

Production rose to five, then seven, then to a magnificent fifteen cars a day.

Sales lagged somewhat behind. Cars were being stocked up, and no one showed any inclination to buy one. The bank balance began to sag, then to plummet. On July 11, 1903, the cash available to the Ford Motor Company was only $223.65. No checks were written on July 12, July 13, or July 14, and morale sagged badly.

The Ford Motor Company would not be the first company to go broke that had started originally with a good idea and good people and what had seemed like a large amount of money ($28,000).

On July 15, Dr. E. Pfenning's letter came with the morning mail. Dr. Pfenning wanted a Ford; his check was enclosed. His car was shipped immediately after his check was deposited. That was the low financial point of the Ford Motor Company; it never again had to worry about cash-on-hand.

But the relief Ford and the others felt when the mail brought order after order in the next few days was short-lived. Less than two weeks after Dr. Pfenning became the first man to buy a Ford-Motor-Company Ford, George Baldwin Selden, the man who had "patented" the automobile, raised his head again.

The newspapers that day carried full-page advertisements, signed by the "Association of Licensed Automobile Manufacturers." The significant part of the ad read, "any person making, selling, or using (unlicensed) machines made or sold by unlicensed manufacturers . . . will be liable to prosecution."

The threat to prosecute buyers or users of "unlicensed" cars was fairly hollow, but there was a little more meat to the threat of prosecuting the manufacturers. Just before this, Smith & Wesson, the gunmakers, had been in a legal suit involving infringement of their patent for loading a revolver from the rear. They had been upheld in court, and other gunmakers who had copied the Smith & Wesson idea had been fined. Through one legal step or another, Smith & Wesson had become the owners of guns made by other people after their patent.

In other words, there was a legal precedent.

Selden, this time, was out of the picture. He had sold, for $10,000, his rights to the patent to the Electric Vehicle Company, a New York City corporation owned by Thomas Fortune Ryan and William C. Whitney. They had formed the company to make, or buy, electric cars for use as taxicabs in Manhattan. They'd had little faith in Selden's patent, but had bought it just to be sure. The Electric Vehicle Company was then worth over $16,000,-000 and the $10,000 they had paid Selden had seemed at the time like cheap insurance.

Once they had the patent, however, they began to have what might be called second thoughts about it. Just to see what would happen, they started a suit for patent infringement against one auto manufacturer. The reaction surprised them; the manufacturer was perfectly willing to pay a reasonable royalty. They started other suits, and one by one, the other manufacturers, except Winton, agreed that they were infringing on the patent and were willing to pay for its use.

Even Winton gave in, just before the suit was to come to trial. Eleven Detroit manufacturers, under the leadership of F. L. Smith of the Olds Motor Company (Olds himself was by now gone) met with Whitney and Ryan in New York and came up with an agreement that they thought solved things nicely all the way around.

Each company would pay to the Association of Licensed Automobile Manufacturers a royalty of 1.25 per cent ($12.50 on a $1,000 car). The association would then pay 60 per cent of the royalty ($7.50 on the same $1,000 car) to the Electric Vehicle Company, keeping the balance for themselves. They could use the money for advertising, for research, for practically anything that would be of mutual interest to all of the manufacturers.

And what really would be to their mutual benefit would be to determine just who could—or could not—manufacture cars. This provision was among the other items in the small print at the bottom of the agreement between Electric Vehicle and the licensed manufacturers.

With two significant exceptions, the licensed manufacturers really represented the industry. In addition to Olds, the renamed Henry Ford Motor Company, now Cadillac, was there. So were Winton, Franklin, Haynes, Apperson, Peerless, Packard, and Pierce-Arrow.

Missing were Thomas Jeffrey, who was making Ramblers in Wisconsin, and the Ford Motor Company.

There are two stories in various histories of the industry about what happened next. One is that Henry Ford applied for membership and was told by F. L. Smith of Olds that he "didn't think an application from Ford would be favorably considered."

That was Mr. Smith's version. The other version is that Smith invited Ford and Couzens to lunch to discuss the enrollment of Ford in the association.

"Mr. Smith," Couzens said, according to this story, "Selden can take his patent and go to hell."

Mr. Smith looked at Mr. Ford, and Mr. Ford said, "You heard Couzens. Take us to court and see what happens."

Henry Ford said he never applied for membership in the association, and he never denied the story of the luncheon meeting.

What the Ford Motor Company did do was take their own advertisements in the newspapers, promising to defend anyone buying one of their cars against any lawsuits brought against them for patent infringement.

The American people have always had a soft spot for the underdog, and Henry Ford knew this. For eight years, while the case against Ford was in court (the court records ultimately filled thirty-eight bound books), Ford very skillfully painted a picture of the poor little Ford Motor Company, who wanted to put an inexpensive car in everyone's garage, bravely battling the assembled forces of the entire industry, who wanted to put him out of business.

In the minds of many people, there was another question. "Why is it that Olds and Packard *really* want to put Ford out of business? Is it possible that a Ford is that much better than their cars?"

Fords really began to sell in large numbers. By the end of 1903, there were a million dollars' worth of Fords on the roads.

CHAPTER VII

The "Big Three" of 1908 were Buick, Ford, and Cadillac, three separate companies. Cadillac sold 2,380 cars that year. Buick was first in sales with 8,485, and Ford was running a close second, with 6,180.

The President of the Buick Motor Company in 1908 was Walter P. Chrysler, who, before he was bitten by the automobile bug, had been works-manager of an even bigger business, the American Locomotive Works. Later, after working for Willys-Overland, he founded the Chrysler Motors Corporation.

His boss was William C. Durant, who had his own ideas about building a huge corporation. He was in favor of one company making all sorts of automobiles at every price range. Durant had an associate, Ben Briscoe, with some money and similar ideas. Briscoe had put up the money to start building Briscoe-Maxwells, soon shortened to Maxwell.

Briscoe and Durant decided that a merger between Maxwell, Reo, Buick, and Ford would be a real money-maker, as indeed it would have been. But when a meeting was called to discuss the matter in detail, Henry Ford and James Couzens asked for $3,000,000. That would have meant that each man would have received an average of $300,000 for his efforts for *each* of the five years the Ford Motor Company had been in business. Olds had his pride too. He demanded $3,000,000 for his Reo Company.

Durant didn't have $50,000, much less a million in cash. Six million dollars was out of the question. The deal fell through.

Briscoe, determined to build a conglomeration of companies, went to the New York banking firm known as the House of Morgan and tried to borrow half a million dollars.

Mr. Morgan did not think highly of Mr. Durant, and cited as proof of Durant's irresponsibility his absolutely "absurd" public statement that one day half a million cars a year would be sold in the United States. No sound banker, he said, would loan such a man a dime.

When they had approached the House of Morgan, Briscoe and Durant had called the company they wanted to form International Motors Corporation. After Morgan turned them down, Briscoe decided to part company with Durant. He told Durant he had no objection if Durant went on his own, but he would prefer that the name International Motors Corporation would not be used. Durant crossed off "International" and "Corporation," kept "Motors" and came up with "General Motors Company."

With $2,000 in cash, William C. Durant incorporated the General Motors Company in New Jersey in 1908. Shortly, and incredibly, he raised the capitalization from $2,000 to $12,500,000. This, of course, is what he, and anyone else he could talk into it, *thought* the company was worth, rather than how it actually appeared on a balance sheet.

Once the corporation had been formed, and the capitalization raised to the twelve-million dollar figure, General Motors acquired Buick for $3,750,250 worth of

The first Chrysler, built in 1924.
CHRYSLER CORPORATION

Walter P. Chrysler (left), one-time Buick President, poses with his chief engineer, Fred Zeder, and the brand-new 1931 Plymouth.   CHRYSLER CORPORATION

General Motors stock, plus $1,500 in cash. Olds Motor Company cost him, a month later, a great deal more money. General Motors became owner of Olds for $17,-279 cash, plus $3,023,574 "worth" of General Motors stock.

But cash was starting to come into the automobile business in amounts beyond anyone's but William C. Durant's imagination. There were first thousands of dollars in the bank, then tens of thousands, and then hundreds of thousands.

In 1908, for example, Durant wanted to buy Cadillac for General Motors. He offered one price, and Wilfred C. Leland, son of the founder and the man who had bought off Henry Ford, countered with an offer of $3,-500,000, with half a million payable immediately in cash. Durant didn't have half a million in cash, and that first deal fell through. Six months later, he tried again. Leland's price was now up to $4,125,000, and he still wanted half a million in cash. Durant still didn't have it.

By the end of 1909, however, Durant had the cash. He paid $500,000, plus $5,169,000 worth of GM stock, and Cadillac joined the firm.

In the same month, Durant tried again to buy Ford. Henry Ford would have taken $3,000,000 the year before. Now he wanted $8,000,000, to be paid $2,000,000 in cash, and the balance in cash, not stock, in two years.

Ford had done about $9,000,000 worth of business in 1908, and earned a $2,700,000 profit; the company expected to make $15,000,000 in 1909. By any standards, except the bankers', it was a good buy. But the bankers

Alfred P. Sloan, Jr. GENERAL MOTORS

were the only ones with money, and they wouldn't advance that large a sum on anything so unpredictable as the horseless carriage. Ford did not join General Motors.

Other companies, a vast and varied assortment of them, did. Some of the auto-manufacturing concerns Durant bought for General Motors (the Randolph and the Ewing for example) died quiet and almost immediate deaths. Others, like the Oakland, which is today's Pontiac Company made General Motors a great deal of money.

Durant was called many things, and the word which seems to fit best is mercurial. Anyone who has even seen mercury running loose on the floor, breaking into smaller lumps, going in all directions at once, has a good idea of Durant's behavior during the formative years of the General Motors Corporation.

With his own money, for example, he financed a French race driver, Albert Champion, who had come up with a new sort of spark plug with a ceramic center. Once it had made money, Durant turned over his 75 per cent interest in what was to become the AC Spark Plug Company to General Motors without making any personal profit from the transaction. But there was another side of Durant's activity too, such as the Haney Lamp Company. About the sole asset of the Haney Company was a patent application for a tungsten lamp. Durant thought this was worth a great deal. He traded $7,000,000 of GM stock for the company, whose patent application was almost immediately turned down by the Patent Office.

Durant had never been highly regarded by the banking profession. He scurried around always trying to raise just enough money to keep in business, and generally just making it. One Buick payroll was paid with money shipped on the railroad from the Buick distributor in New England; there was no money in the Buick account in Detroit, and the Detroit bankers were unwilling to loan Durant enough money to pay his workers.

In 1910–1911, Durant was really in trouble. Swallowing his pride, he was able to borrow money from Boston and New York banking firms on the condition that he permit a sort of trusteeship of bankers to run the company. It was the same sort of arrangement, more or less as that by which financier Howard Hughes was forced to turn over management of TWA to ostensibly more solid, wiser businessmen.

The bankers did not assume management of General Motors out of an interest for their fellow man. They loaned GM $12,750,000 at 6 per cent interest. In other words GM got $12,750,000 in cash, and agreed to pay back $15,000,000. For their efforts, the bankers received $6,169,200 in GM stock.

There was virtually no risk. The loan was guaranteed by the real property of GM. If Durant had gone completely broke, it could have been sold for a good deal more than $15,000,000.

Henry Ford, who was never very fond of bankers, watched the proceedings with great interest. He watched how much money was being taken by the bankers, and he watched how William C. Durant, without whom there would have been no General Motors at all, was demoted to a vice-presidency and stripped of all his authority.

Durant was down, but not quite out.

He had always been fascinated with European race drivers, and now he had two; still another pair of brothers, Louis and Arthur Chevrolet. Durant had them race against each other. Arthur lost, because he had taken no chances.

Louis won. He was put to work in the Buick factory designing a car to bear his name. Arthur went to work as William C. Durant's chauffeur; he liked drivers who took no chances.

The Haney Lamp Company blunder had not exactly displeased stockholders of the Haney Lamp Company. If it had not been for Durant, they would have been holding shares of stock in a worthless company. Because of him, they now held shares of GM.

Apparently on the belief that a man who had saved him several million dollars couldn't be all bad, a New York banker who had owned Haney stock quietly advanced Durant enough money to gain control of Chevrolet. Durant immediately offered GM stockholders a very profitable swap: five shares of Chevrolet for one GM.

The Chevrolet was an immediate success. GM stockholders were perfectly willing to take its stock at a five-to-one ratio. In 1915, William C. Durant, who controlled Chevrolet, which owned a little better than half of all GM stock, walked into the Board Room and announced, in effect, that he was back.

He was going to vote Chevrolet's stock, more than 51 per cent and Chevrolet was going to vote for W. C. Durant for President of GM. The bankers muttered in their beards, but there wasn't anything that could be done about it.

GM was making money, and it was suddenly provided with more, in 1915–1917, through the efforts of John Jacob Raskob, treasurer of the DuPont Company. DuPont bought about 29 per cent of GM stock and Raskob, for a change, was a financier who thought that Durant should be allowed to wheel and deal.

Durant bought the Fisher Body Company, and, for $56,000 (now small change to him), the Guardian Frigerator Company. It was renamed Frigidaire, and quickly put to work cooling the nation's food.

He made one more magnificent acquisition, before his day was over.

In Newark, New Jersey, at the turn of the century, there was a small metal working company known as the Hyatt Roller Bearing Company. It made bearings for industry, particularly the sugar industry, and did so on the verge of financial disaster.

John Wesley Hyatt, who had founded the company, was experimenting with something new. While trying to invent a substitute for ivory billiard balls, he invented celluloid—in other words, the plastic industry.

The company was so badly run that a very young man, Alfred P. Sloan, Jr., who had only gone to work there a few years before, was able to talk his father into advancing him the princely sum of $5,000 to give him control of the business. Under Sloan's hand, the company started to make a little money, but not very much.

In 1899, however, when Elwood Haynes wrote his letter from Kokomo, business began to boom. Haynes wanted bearings for his automobile. Hyatt provided them. Then Ransom E. Olds wanted bearings. Then Ford. And Cadillac, and just about everyone else making cars.

In 1916, Alfred P. Sloan had a call from Durant. How much would he take for the company?

He said he wanted $15,000,000. Roughly, that meant that Hyatt had grown in worth by $1 million a year each year since Sloan had taken it over. Hyatt was at that time selling to both sides of the competition, and he knew that it was only a matter of time before either Ford or GM decided it would be cheaper to make their own.

In other words, if he didn't go with GM, it was obvious that GM would start making its own bearings, and then Ford would have him in a bad position.

The price agreed upon was $13,500,000, half in cash and half in stock in a GM subsidiary, United Motors Corporation, a sort of holding company that owned many of the companies supplying GM with its parts.

Sloan's father, and the others who had loaned him the $5,000 to take over Hyatt, now wanted cash for their part of it. Sloan wound up with little cash and a great chunk of stock in United Motors, so much stock that he announced he was now the President of United Motors.

Durant got along quite well with Sloan personally, and decided that he would place Sloan where he could keep an eye on him as a bright young man for the future. It was to Sloan's financial advantage to permit United Motors to be absorbed by GM. This was done, and Sloan was elected Vice-President of General Motors.

For Billy Durant, that was the high point, and then things started to go downward.

Walter Chrysler, President of Buick, finally had the last of a long series of verbal brawls with Durant. He stormed out, announcing that he was going to show Durant what he could do at the head of a company bearing his own name.

Henry Leland of Cadillac also had his last disagreement with Durant, and he too quit, taking a comfortable number of millions with him.

The post-World War I boom, which had made everybody money, collapsed right at this time. Durant tried to save the company's stock, to keep its price high, by using his own money. It was a good try, but it wasn't good enough. He ran out of money. The DuPonts stepped in and made the necessary money available, both to save their own investment, and to spare the country the financial trouble that the collapse of GM would mean. Durant turned over 2,500,000 shares of his stock to the DuPonts, announced his resignation, and left the company, just about as broke as he had been when he started it.

Pierre DuPont became President, but in practice he left the management to Alfred P. Sloan. The DuPont-GM relationship was to last until after World War II, when the courts forced the DuPont company to divest itself of all GM stock in an anti-trust suit.

Durant tried to build his own cars, and for a little while succeeded, but the 1929 depression rolled over him too. He filed a petition for bankruptcy in 1935, listing some 200-odd dollars in assets, and $914,000 in liabilities.

CHAPTER VIII

Ford traditionally has had the reputation for making low-priced cars. Because Henry Ford always believed that more people would buy inexpensive cars, and ultimately, he would make more money that way.

Up until 1906, his idea of making a car, which he called "universal," or one that would be all things to all people, caused a problem with Malcolmson. In addition to the small Fords being manufactured, the Ford Motor Company was selling a Model K, a plush automobile, which competed roughly with Cadillac. It sold for $2,800 and the company lost money on every sale. Malcolmson said this was necessary, because the Model K gave the entire Ford line some prestige. Ford wanted to stop selling the Model K completely, and the fact that it was losing money seemed to prove his argument.

There was merit on both sides. It is generally accepted today, for example, that manufacturers lose money on flashy convertibles, but they are perfectly willing to do so because of the "image" the convertible gives the rest of the line. A man who comes into a show room to look at a flaming red convertible is likely to buy a more sedate version of the car, and still be able to think of himself as a sort of "swinger."

Malcolmson, however, had left his man Couzens in charge of his interest in the Ford Motor Company, and devoted his efforts to keeping the coal business going. When it became apparent that the Ford Motor Company was growing by leaps and bounds, Malcolmson tried to change his mind, and assume leadership of the automobile company. Couzens and Ford would have none of this.

Together with the Dodge Brothers, they formed the Ford Manufacturing Company. The Ford Manufacturing Company sold the parts from which the Ford Motor Company built its cars. The books were arranged so that the price paid for the parts was all credited to the Ford Manufacturing Company. Couzens, the Dodges and Ford, in other words, took all the profits, while the Ford Motor Company just kept its financial head out of the water.

Malcolmson realized that he had no choice but to sell out. He sold his share of the Ford Motor Company to Henry Ford for $175,000 in July of 1906. The other initial partners, Bennett, Fry, Strelow, the carpenter who built the first plant, and Woodall left soon afterward, taking what they thought at the time to be more than a fair price for their shares, and leaving Henry Ford and Couzens to their madness.

When this reshuffle was over, Couzens held 110 shares and Ford 585, with 315 more shares in the hands of other people. Ford, without question, had control of the Ford Motor Company. As soon as he had absolute control, he stopped making the Model K, and began developing the car which would be the Model T.

It was not a thing of beauty, although, to many people, it was a joy nearly forever. It was simple and rugged. There was no water pump; water circulated because water at different temperatures will move. Fuel feed was by

107

The 1903 Model A Ford. FORD MOTOR COMPANY

The 1905 Model C Ford. FORD MOTOR COMPANY

The 1907 Model R Ford. FORD MOTOR COMPANY

gravity; there was no fuel pump. The Model T had a four-cylinder engine developing twenty horsepower, and, when the wind was right, the Model T would make about forty miles per hour. Ford decided that it was more important for the driver to see how close he would be to a car coming in the other direction than to see how close he was to the curb, and moved the steering wheel to the left side of the car.

It was designed for the roads of the day, which meant that while it wasn't especially smooth-riding, neither did it often become stuck in the mud. The suspension system provided for an almost incredible flexibility; the Model T could go where cars today wouldn't dare attempt to drive, and there are a number of people familiar with both vehicles who say that it could travel just about anywhere a jeep can travel.

There were three pedals on the floor. The throttle was a lever on the steering-wheel column about where the gearshift lever is today. Beside the left hand of the driver was a lever, sticking out of the floorboard.

It was started with a crank, mounted permanently beneath the radiator, which now bore the familiar Ford name in flowing script. The throttle (or accelerator) was opened a little by moving the lever on the steering-wheel column. The spark was adjusted with another level. The driver spun the crank. And spun the crank. And spun the crank. Eventually, but inevitably, the engine would catch, and shake and gasp and sputter until the driver could race around the side of the car, leap behind the wheel, and toy with the throttle and spark levers until the engine smoothed down a bit.

The hand lever had three positions. All the way back was in "emergency brake" position. Straight up and down was in neutral, and all the way forward, in high speed.

With the engine running and the hand-lever straight-up (in neutral), the engine was revved by pulling down on the throttle lever. At the same time, the hand lever was thrown forward, and the far-left floor pedal was stepped on. The Ford would then move forward in low gear. When it was moving, the driver let up the pressure on the foot pedal, and the transmission automatically shifted into high. He could let his foot rest until he had to slow (the brake pedal was on the right). The center pedal was reverse. It was possible to go directly from high to reverse, and some drivers used this characteristic of the Ford instead of the brakes.

Ford called his transmission "planetary." As crude as it was, not only did it work well, but it served as the basic principle for automatic transmissions, which came after the clutch system.

The first Model T, or perhaps more accurately, the Model T put on sale in 1908 wasn't, by a long shot, the cheapest car on the road. Sears, Roebuck, for example, was selling its own cars, with the stripped model priced at $395, and the deluxe (with top, side curtains and "storm" front) for $495. Ford asked $850 for the Model T, and this price did not include such luxury options as a spare tire and wheel, a top, a windshield, or headlights.

These were available at extra cost to those with money to burn.

The customer had a choice between a red touring car (front and back seats) or a gray roadster (single seat). Eventually, after making some cars available in a dark green, Henry Ford decided in 1909 that black was the color a car should be painted. All Fords thereafter were painted black.

In 1909, the American automobile industry produced somewhere around 124,000 cars. Not quite 19,000 of these were Fords, which is to say the Model T, because that was all Ford was making. Four years later, in 1913, Ford manufactured a quarter of a million Model T's, which was nearly 40 per cent of the total production of the country. In 1921, the company manufactured a million Model T's, and two years after that, two million.

The car was good, and so was the method of distribution and service. Ford designed the car so that it would be easy to repair. He made parts available at low prices, and he made them widely available. A Ford dealership, obviously, was a very good way to get rich, but those aspiring to a dealership found that they would get rich according to Mr. Ford's ideas, and not any of their own.

Ford insisted that each Ford dealer carry a large, complete stock of parts. And he set the price the dealer could charge for each part. If the customer preferred to have the dealer replace a muffler (two dollars) instead of replacing it himself, he found that Ford had set the price the dealer could charge for that service, too: sixty cents.

He set rules for the location of Ford showrooms, for their standards of cleanliness, and even for how the cars could be advertised.

The demand for the cars grew. The Ford factory area grew, and the number of employees, but Ford was convinced that the answer to increased production was not simply increased facilities and employees, but more efficient use of the employees and facilities already on hand.

In his autobiography, he said that he got the idea for the assembly line from a visit he paid to the meat-processing plant of a Chicago packer. If a carcass could be reduced to steaks, chops, and roasts as it moved down a line of workers, Henry Ford decided that the reverse was probably true. A car could be efficiently assembled by going past a line of workers.

He started first with the flywheel magneto. This part, turned by the flywheel, generated electric power. Working alone at a bench, a workman could assemble between thirty-five and forty magnetos during one (then standard) nine-hour day. Each assembly took him about twenty minutes.

Ford engineers watched the assembler, and saw that there were twenty-nine separate steps in the assembly of the magneto; twenty-nine parts to put together, tighten, adjust, and so on.

Some of the operations were closely allied. In other words, the worker could put two parts together, and then two more parts, because the work was right in front of his hands, and there was no wasted motion. Other oper-

*The Ford 1908 Model T
Touring Car.*
FORD ARCHIVES

*The 1909 Ford Model T
Roadster.* FORD MOTOR COMPANY

ations, the work analysts saw, were not related. The workman had to turn around and leave his bench, pick something up, put a tool down and get another tool.

A production line was set up. Assembly of the magneto was broken down into steps, with a workman doing the same thing over and over to different magnetos, rather than all the different operations to one magneto before moving on to the next.

Instead of the workman going to the magneto, it was brought to him on a moving belt. The belt moved just fast enough for each workman to do his part of the assembly before it carried the magneto to the next workman.

The idea worked. It had taken twenty minutes of labor to build one magneto. The first production line cut this to thirteen minutes, ten seconds. In 1914, the work analysts raised the height of the work area six inches, and this cut assembly time to seven minutes. Further refinements cut assembly time per magneto to five minutes.

Phrased another way, that meant that one man was doing in 1915 what four men had done in 1909.

With highly skilled, experienced workmen, three or four working at a time, it had taken twelve hours and twenty-eight minutes to assemble one chassis when the method of production was to bring the parts to the chassis as needed and bolt them on.

The first chassis assembly line had the chassis being pulled down an assembly line by ropes. The parts to go on the chassis were stacked along the line, which was 256 feet long. A team of six assemblers would join the bare chassis at the start of the line, and walk down the line with it, assembling it from parts they picked up on their way. This was a rough experiment, but it cut work hours to five hours and fifty minutes per chassis—less than half the manpower required under the old system.

A more efficient system of moving the chassis came next, and one refinement after another, such as the precise height the line should be. It reached the point where one assembly line was for short men, and one for taller ones. The whole idea was to eliminate wasted motion.

Ultimately, from twelve hours and twenty-eight minutes of labor per chassis, the time was cut to one hour and thirty-three minutes. In six months in 1913, the assembly line had cut assembly time of the engine from nine hours and fifty-four minutes to five hours and fifty-six minutes.

Ford was able to make his cars ever more cheaply. By 1914, the price to the customer was down from $850 to $490; in 1924, the all-time low, a customer with $290 could drive off in a brand-new Ford in any color of his choice, as long as he liked black.

The lower the price went, the more people bought cars. And the money rolled in.

Between 1906 and 1910, the Ford Motor Company showed profits of $25,000,000 (58.5 per cent of which, of course, went into Henry Ford's pocket). Stockholders began getting dividends rather frequently; for a while, there was a check each quarter, for 15 per cent. Then there were special dividends (30 per cent, 100 per cent, and finally 500 per cent, a dividend of $10,000,000). On that one dividend payment alone Henry Ford grew $5,-850,000 richer.

Henry Ford started the new year of 1914 in a way that flabbergasted and wholly delighted his employees and outraged just about every other businessman in the country. On January 4, 1914, he called a press conference. When the reporters showed up, they found Couzens ready to read a prepared announcement while Henry Ford sat in a corner of the room watching the proceedings.

It was something less than a modest and self-effacing statement. Couzens read that, "The Ford Motor Company, the greatest and most successful automobile-manufacturing company in the world will, on January 12, inaugurate the greatest revolution in the matter of rewards for its workers ever known to the industrial world. At one stroke it will reduce the hours of work from nine to eight."

At that point there were audible gasps from the reporters. Couzens stopped and gave them time to adjust to this amazing gift to labor—there had been no strike, not even unrest. Ford employees seemed to be happy as Ford employees, yet Ford was cutting their work by more than 10 per cent, which was the same thing as saying that he was increasing their wages that much. At $2.34 per eight-hour day, Ford was paying the highest wages in industry.

When the rustle had died down, Couzens continued: "The smallest sum to be received by any one man twenty-two years and upward will be five dollars a day."

A cutaway view of the planetary transmission and magneto of the Model T Ford.   FORD ARCHIVES

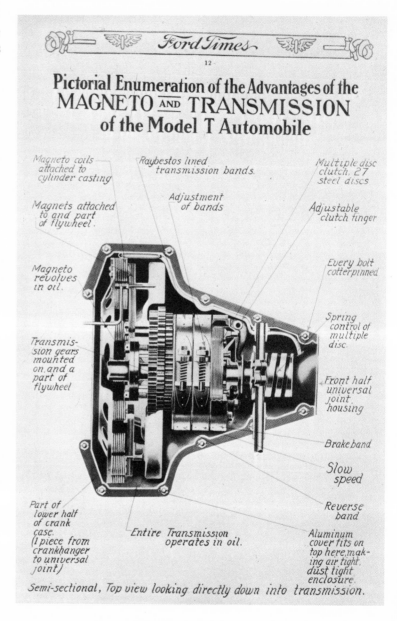

Ford Times
12

Pictorial Enumeration of the Advantages of the MAGNETO AND TRANSMISSION of the Model T Automobile

Magneto coils attached to cylinder casting

Raybestos lined transmission bands.

Multiple disc clutch, 27 steel discs

Magnets attached to and part of flywheel.

Adjustment of bands

Adjustable clutch finger

Magneto revolves in oil.

Every bolt cotterpinned

Transmission gears mounted on, and a part of flywheel

Spring control of multiple disc.

Front half universal joint housing

Brake band

Slow speed

Part of lower half of crank case. (1 piece from crankhanger to universal joint)

Entire Transmission operates in oil.

Reverse band

Aluminum cover fits on top here, making air tight, dust tight enclosure.

Semi-sectional, Top view looking directly down into transmission.

He was doubling the wages to an incredible five dollars a day.

The competition, other industrialists, and bankers were literally sputtering with rage. Ford was obviously a madman, bent in wrecking the established order of things. The workers would take the extra money and stay drunk; it wouldn't work.

The *Wall Street Journal* made fun of him while the Socialist party, on the other extreme, condemned him. They didn't know what he was up to, but it was obviously some capitalist trick.

The Ford workers just pocketed the money and kept working.

There was now, however, the beginning of internal dissent in the Ford Motor Company. Henry Ford, seeing that he had indeed put America on wheels, and was certainly the most enlightened employer in the history of mankind, began to act as if he had answers for the rest of the world's problems as well. He demontrated little patience with anyone who dared disagree with him. Henry Ford became rather difficult to get along with.

The Dodge Brothers had it out with him. It must have been one of the classic brawls of all time, but no one was there with a tape recorder or a television camera to record it, so all we know is that the Dodge Brothers cancelled their contract to supply Ford Motor Company with parts, and left the company, taking with them their Ford Motor Company stock.

Next to go was Couzens himself. It was Henry Ford's firm and oft-spoken belief that the United States had no business whatever in taking sides in the war then being fought in Europe. It was none of our business, he said, and we should keep out of it.

He commanded a great deal of personal prestige. Anyone who could get to be *that* rich, reasoned many Americans, obviously had to be smart. He made at least as much sense as most politicians did, people trusting politicians in 1915 no more than they do today.

Couzens quit in 1915, citing Ford's views on peace, the Allies' War Loan (Henry Ford had made it plain that any American who supported loaning the French and the English any money must be crazy), and National Preparedness. (Henry Ford was not exactly against self-defense. But he had asked what were the chances of the Kaiser invading New York when he couldn't get as far as the English Channel.)

In 1916, Henry Ford announced that there would be no more dividends for a while. He was going to build an even larger factory (to be by far the world's largest) at River Rouge. Raw materials would go in one side of River Rouge and Fords would come out the other. He needed the money to build River Rouge. He had no intention of going to any banker and asking for a loan.

The Dodge Brothers took him to court. They pleaded that they were entitled to a return on their investment. The Court supported them, and Ford was ordered to declare a dividend. He dutifully instructed his new treasurer, the man who had replaced Couzens, to pay the dividend. It was for $19,000,000.

But he had no intention of permitting a situation to exist in which he could be told what to do.

He went to California, called a press conference, and announced that he was leaving the Ford Motor Company to start a new company, which he and his son Edsel would own outright. The new company would design, manufacture, and sell a new car, which would be cheaper and better in every way than the current Ford. He didn't know, nor much care, he said, what was going to happen to the old Ford Motor Company, and he was not in the market for any of the stock he didn't happen to own.

It might have been an idle threat, but no one cared to call his bluff. He had the money to do just about anything he wanted to do. About $12,000,000 of the $19,-000,000 court-ordered dividend, for example, had been paid to Henry Ford as a stockholder.

When the first shock tremors had passed, the other stockholders gave in. Through intermediaries, Ford bought up all the outstanding stock. Couzens received $29,308,857.90. The estate of Banker Gray, the man who had come up with the $10,500 dollars to pay the Dodge boys at the beginning, got $26,250,000. The Dodge brothers themselves shared $25,000,000. John W. Anderson, whose initial investment had been $5,000 got a check for $12,500,000. Bennett H. Rackham, who had invested a total of $10,500, also got $12,500,000.

Henry and Edsel Ford now owned the Ford Motor Company outright.

CHAPTER IX Henry Leland, who had taken over the Henry Ford Company from Henry Ford and seen it renamed Cadillac after the French explorer, was by training, education and interest a machinist. He'd learned his trade at the Springfield Arsenal making firearms, and had worked for Colt. Firearms, like automobiles, are made of steel, machined to fine tolerances. Because of military requirements, efforts had always been made, with varying degrees of success, to make parts interchangeable between guns.

The pistol with which our servicemen have been armed for more than half a century is called the U. S. Pistol, Caliber .45 M1911A1. It's more popularly known as the Colt automatic, and its history goes back to the Philippine Insurrection, right after the turn of the century, at the time of the birth of the automobile.

From time to time, tribesmen in the Philippines would take one or more narcotics, and then head for the nearest American soldier, swinging a machete. The Army at that time had a .38 caliber revolver, which did not prove effective enough against these attacks. A new bullet was required, and while the Army was looking for it, they also announced a contest for a new standard pistol.

The Moro tribesmen had been pacified by General Arthur MacArthur, the father of General Douglas MacArthur, long before the Army settled on a new pistol and a new bullet. The new bullet was .45 caliber, or .45 inch, and weighed 230 grains. Its man-stopping ability has only in recent years been challenged. The new gun was a self-loader, which means that when the trigger is pulled,

122

and the gun discharged, it also cocks the gun again, and puts a fresh bullet in the chamber.

The gun was a refinement of a self-loading pistol developed about 1900 by John Moses Browning, a Utah gunsmith and the greatest firearms genius in history. It was obviously a major step forward in firearms, not only because it worked so well, but because its parts could be replaced, easily and anywhere, by anyone armed with the gun. A gunsmith was not needed in every unit.

For parts to be interchangeable, great precision was required. When Leland left the Arsenal and then Colt's employ, he was a master machinist and a great believer in precision. He was the first American to import a set of measuring blocks, called "Jo Blocks" after their inventor, Swedish engineer Carl Johansson. These measuring tools were accurate within 4 millionths of an inch (.000004 inch).

Leland didn't make Cadillacs quite that precisely, but he made them far more precisely than anyone else had ever made an automobile. In 1908 he announced that, like the parts of a Springfield rifle or a Colt pistol, any part on any Cadillac could be exchanged for any part on any other Cadillac. And then he proved this to the frankly skeptical Royal Automobile Club in England.

Three Cadillacs were stripped by British mechanics as officials watched. The pile of parts was stirred around to mix them, and eighty-nine new parts were placed in the pile. Then the eighty-nine parts from the disassembled Cadillacs were removed.

Henry Leland. GENERAL MOTORS

The cars were then reassembled by American mechanics, while the British made sure that no effort was made to match two parts that had been together before. The cars were started up, and driven five hundred miles. They functioned perfectly, and Leland won the Dewar Trophy for an outstanding contribution to the art of automobiling.

If Cadillac could do it, the other manufacturers at least had to try. (Henry Ford finally bought out the Johansson Company from under Leland's nose, making Ford the sole proprietor of the measuring blocks.) The automobile quickly ceased to be something made by hand and became something machined.

There was no established organization for automobiles as there was, for example, for chemical engineering, or structural engineering, or even electrical engineering, so the automobile people formed the Society of Automobile Engineers. It was started half tongue-in-cheek because there really were no criteria to define an automotive engineer. The founder, E. T. Birdsall, said that membership would have to be open to "anyone who could recognize, at sight, an automobile on Fifth Avenue."

It wasn't quite that informal, of course. The first president of the SAE was A. L. Riker, chief engineer of Locomobile. Henry Ford was the first vice-president.

It was a place where the experimentors could share knowledge, and a forum for new ideas. In a practical sense, the SAE began to establish standards for the automotive industry, so that, for example, a manufacturer

124

The first Cadillac, built in 1903. GENERAL MOTORS

wanting to buy 100,000 bolts from a bolt manufacturer could specify the SAE type and get bolts which would be the proper ones for the purpose intended. And they standardized the parts they were already using.

In 1910, for example, an SAE study showed that more than eight hundred different sizes and types of lockwashers were being used. The study further showed that only sixteen sizes were really needed to supply the demands of everyone in the business. The same sort of simplification was applied wherever possible. The SAE is still a strong factor in the automobile business today; its standards are recognized world-wide as the most practical and accurate.

In 1911, a man named Charles Franklin Kettering made his major contribution to the automobile. Kettering began his engineering career while a student at Ohio State University. He paid his own way with money earned in the summers installing switchboards and serving as a general repairman for the local telephone company.

When he graduated from college, he went to work for the National Cash Register Company and invented the electric motor that opens cash register drawers. He became involved with automobiles in a rather round-about way. He was friendly with his boss's secretary, and when she left National Cash Register to go to work for Leland at Cadillac, he kept in touch with her.

Leland was dissatisfied with the ignition system of the Cadillac. Like most cars of the day, it had a double source of power. Half a dozen dry-cell batteries, wired

126

in series, provided the spark to start the engine, and to keep it running at low speed. Beyond a certain speed, a magneto could be operated. A magneto is a rather simple device that, when cranked, provides an electrical current. They're still in use in some motorcycles, on piston aircraft engines and on military-field telephones.

Dry-cell batteries would provide spark for ignition for about two hundred miles, and then went dead. Furthermore, a switch to go from battery to magneto and back was necessary.

Kettering devised an electrical circuit which, in effect, saved up electrical power and then delivered it all at once, in a fat spark, rather than in a steady flow of power as before. His invention increased battery life by ten times, and just about eliminated the need for a magneto at all.

Through his boss's secretary, he got the idea before Leland at Cadillac, who bought it and tried to hire Kettering away from National Cash Register. Kettering was unwilling to work for Cadillac, but he thought he should set out on his own. His boss at National Cash Register, E. A. Deeds, gave him the use of his barn in Dayton, Ohio, and Kettering, gathering around him a few men with similar ideas, formed a company that, considering their barn, had a rather elegant title: Dayton Engineering Laboratories Company. It soon became known as DELCO.

In 1910, a friend of Cadillac's Henry Leland died of a broken jaw. Gallantly, he had stopped to help that rare creature, a lady motorist, whose car had stalled. Few

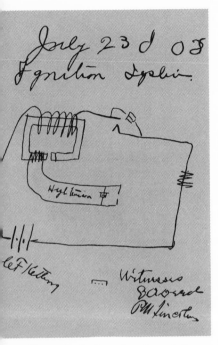

Kettering's first drawing of the self-starter circuit, July 23, 1908.
GENERAL MOTORS

women had either the strength or the courage to crank a car. He'd wound the crank for her, her car had backfired, and the crank had caught his jaw and broken it.

The crank was dangerous and everyone knew it, but there didn't seem to be a solution. The electrical engineers had studied the problem of a self-starter and concluded that, while it was possible, it was not feasible.

It would take an electric motor generating five horsepower to effectively start an automobile engine. A motor that large, along with the size and weight of the batteries necessary to turn the starting motor, would weigh just about what the car itself weighed, and take up about 90 per cent of its usable space.

The mathematics of the electrical engineers was faultless, but Kettering thought he saw a flaw in their reasoning. They were talking about a motor which would turn over the engine *for an indefinite period.* All that was required was to turn it over for a few seconds, until the engine caught. It wasn't really too much different from the motor he'd designed for the cash register drawer. If the motor didn't have to run continuously, it could be overloaded.

Leland told Kettering that if he could make such a motor, he'd buy at least four thousand of them. Kettering set to work, and came up with a system that not only provided a starter motor for the gasoline engine, but a generator, which, when the gasoline engine was running, recharged the battery and provided a source of electrical power for headlamps.

128

The first self-starter appeared on the 1912 Cadillac. It worked, and Kettering was asked to address the Society of Electrical Engineers in Detroit, to explain how he had solved the insurmountable problem. When he'd finished, a highly irate electrical engineer stood up and demanded to know why they had permitted a man to address their group who had "profaned every fundamental law of electrical engineering." It is said that the phrase "he cried all the way to the bank" was coined at this time to describe Kettering's feelings for having been accused of "profaning" the laws of electrical engineering.

Once he had what he thought of as enough money, Kettering was happy to go on experimenting almost for the sake of experimentation. He sold controlling interest in DELCO to United Motors because he didn't want to bother with the worry of running a business. United Motors was in turn owned by GM, and GM wanted Kettering to leave Ohio and come to Detroit to head up a new company, the General Motors Research Company.

Charles Franklin Kettering
GENERAL MOTORS

Kettering said no. He didn't want to go to Detroit to do anything. He liked what he was doing, and he liked doing it in Ohio.

The men who wanted him to head the Research Company were William C. Durant, Pierre S. DuPont (of DuPont), John Jacob Raskob (the DuPont financial genius), Alfred P. Sloan (formerly of Hyatt Roller Bearing), and Walter P. Chrysler. To a man, they were not known for taking "no" as a final answer. But they had never before encountered a man like Charles Franklin Kettering either.

The first Franklin automobile was sold in 1902 to S. G. Auerall, shown at the wheel.
NATIONAL ARCHIVES

The 1969 Chevrolet Corvair Monza. This air-cooled engine car, too, failed.
GENERAL MOTORS

Finally, he proposed terms that seem fantastic. He would come to Detroit, he said, and do research for them, but he wanted it clearly understood that he was to have no authority, no responsibility. They would give him all the money he wanted, and furthermore, never ask him any questions about what he'd done with it.

Otherwise, he'd stay in Ohio.

They granted him his terms, and he promptly embarked on what people considered his only failure.

With one exception, the Franklin, all automobile engines were water-cooled. Their blocks were constructed with passages for water around the cylinders and exhaust manifolds. They required water pumps, plumbing, hoses, and radiators. Water rusted the block, hoses leaked, pumps failed, radiators overheated, and they were, it was generally conceded, a mess.

The Franklin was air-cooled. Its cylinders were vaned, that is, they were cast in such a way that closely spaced vanes surrounded them, very much as if someone had taken a saw and sawed almost through the cylinder again and again, the width of a saw blade part. This increased the surface of the cylinder many times over. Heat was transferred to the vanes, and it was then dissipated into the air.

(Aircraft engines have pistons of this type, and long after the Franklin Automobile Company went broke, aircraft-engine manufacturers were paying royalties to the Franklin Company for the use of their idea.)

General Motors couldn't manufacture Franklinlike engines without paying Franklin large royalties, and even if they had been willing to pay the royalties, manufacturing as many engines as GM would need posed problems of its own.

Kettering, both to get around the Franklin patent, and to improve upon the idea, set to work on an engine which would have a standard cast-iron cylinder and copper vanes, or fins.

Copper and cast iron have what the engineers call a different coefficient of linear expansion; they expand at different rates when heated.

Pierre S. DuPont who heretofore had left the management of GM almost entirely to Sloan, became a strong advocate of the copper engine. He thought that Kettering was right—that an engine of the kind he was developing would indeed revolutionize the engine industry. He backed Kettering with all of his awesome influence. It reached the point where the 1923 Chevrolet was unveiled with a copper-jacketed engine at the annual Auto Show. It was a sensation, and 759 actually were made.

They didn't work. They overheated, froze up mechanically, and came apart. Alfred P. Sloan who, following Durant's departure, was at that time running General Motors, ordered the cars recalled and scrapped.

Kettering went to him, resignation in hand. He still maintained he was on the right track, and if GM didn't want his idea, he'd go to someone else who did.

He was a genius, but he was outwitted by Alfred P. Sloan. It would be unnecessary for Kettering to quit,

132

Sloan said. If Kettering felt that the idea was sound, GM had enough faith in Kettering not only to agree with him, but to set up a whole new division, adequately finance it, and turn it over to Kettering to make his new copper-jacketed-engine automobile. There was only one small catch: They didn't have anyone to spare to handle the administration of the new division, nor to handle promotion or sales of the new car. Kettering would have to do that by himself.

That was the last heard of the copper-jacketed engine. GM didn't get around to an air-cooled engine again until the Corvair, 1959–1969.

The air-cooled, copper-jacketed engine was not the only thing that Kettering had been working on in his laboratories. Since 1916, he'd been working on knock. We are all now able very knowledgeably to refer to knock as predetonation, but Kettering was the man who discovered what it was.

It posed some problems. It was there—there was no question about that. Engines knocked. They seemed to knock more, embarrassingly enough, with Kettering's coil-ignition system than they did with the old magneto. But what caused it? The obvious answer was to look inside the cylinder and see what was knocking.

That in itself posed a great many problems, because steel is not transparent. Glass, which is transparent, shatters when subjected to the pressure of a cylinder full of exploding gasoline vapor.

Kettering and his assistant, Tom Midgely, first solved

the problem of looking into a cylinder. (Kettering refused to have subordinates. Anyone who worked with him he called an "associate." He was quoted as saying that the only rank in his laboratories was when one man happened to be ranker than another. Midgely was proud to refer to himself as "Boss Kett's assistant.")

They polished a thick piece of quartz, and devised a method of putting this into a cylinder wall. They could see the gasoline vapor detonate, and they could hear the knock. It told them nothing.

Kettering then proceeded to invent high-speed photography. He took a tomato-juice can and wrapped a sheet of film around it, holding it in place with rubber bands. The can was spun rapidly and Midgely worked a high-speed shutter. That added the speed of the revolving drum to the speed of the shutter, and they came up with split-second pictures of what happened inside the cylinder.

They saw that there were really two explosions, and found out what this meant. It had to do with the quality, or volatility, of gasoline.

Around the turn of the century, gasoline had been an unpopular, even unwanted, product of the petroleum industry.

All petroleum is made up of carbon and hydrogen, arranged in different sizes and arrangements of molecules. The smaller the molecules, the more volatile the product. Crude oil was refined by heating it, and then collecting the resulting vapor. When crude oil was processed around the turn of the century, the first product to turn to vapor

134

was gasoline, because it has the smallest molecular structure. Then came kerosene, with slightly larger molecules, then the various grades of fuel oil, then lubricating oil, then heavy lubricants.

Before the automobile, there was little or no demand for gasoline. When crude oil was refined, far more gasoline was thrown into rivers than sold. Kerosene was what the public wanted, and the government used to station kerosene inspectors in the refineries to make sure that the refiners didn't try to cheat by mixing gasoline with the valuable kerosene.

The result of this was that the first motorists to get gasoline got a very high quality product, the most volatile possible, because the refiners turned the valve and mixed less volatile gasoline with the kerosene.

When the demand for gasoline increased at about the same time that the electric light was lowering the demand for kerosene for lamps, the reverse happened. The refiners mixed as much less valuable kerosene with gasoline as they could get away with.

What was causing a knock in the cylinder of gasoline engines was this difference in volatility and molecular structure. The small molecules of gasoline would immediately detonate from the spark at the spark plug, but the larger molecules of kerosene were not volatile enough to be detonated by the spark. They were detonated a fraction of a second later by the flame from the exploding gasoline.

There was only so much gasoline available, even after

1913, when Dr. William Burton of Standard Oil found a way to "crack" the very heavy molecular structure of oil into gasoline-like molecules in a heating process. What Kettering had to do was find a way to increase the volatility of what gasoline there was. Otherwise, engines would knock themselves to pieces.

Kettering reasoned that since dark colors absorb heat, it might be that if he dyed gasoline a darker color, the heavier molecules would absorb enough heat from the lighter molecules so that both molecular structures would detonate at once.

They mixed iodine with the fuel, and the knock disappeared. But so did the walls of the cylinder, the rings and the piston. Iodine was corrosive. But the idea apparently was sound.

Iodine is a natural element. Kettering reasoned that if one natural element was a knock-suppressant, another might be too. He found that aniline worked very well, but that it caused such a smell that the car they were testing it in was known around the laboratory as "The Goat."

Finally, they found tetraethyl lead. It worked. About 90 per cent of the gasoline sold today contains tetraethyl lead. There was a bonus to this discovery. Lead gasoline burned smoothly under high compression, which meant that more useable energy could be obtained from the same amount of gas.

Before ethyl, the compression ratio of automobile engines couldn't get much above 4.5:1. Compression ratio is the relationship between the volume of fuel mixture taken into the cylinder and the volume of the same mixture at the instant of detonation, when the piston is at the upper limit of its travel.

Once Kettering had found the cure for knock, the compression ratio jumped almost immediately to 6:1. A high-compression engine in an automobile of today has a ratio of 11:1, and the ratio continues to go slightly higher all the time.

Kettering put color on cars too.

When Henry Ford announced that his customers could have any color they wanted so long as it was black, it wasn't just one more manifestation of his firm belief that he knew what was best for everybody, but rather the obvious solution to the otherwise insoluble problem of painting vast numbers of cars.

Enamel, available only in black and a few other, even less joyous colors, such as flat gray, had a characteristic that made it indispensable to mass production. It could be dried in two hours, if the car was put in a 400° oven. Even that time seemed to be excessive, and Ford spent vast amounts of money trying to find a better method of painting his cars, primarily to speed up the process.

A red, or light blue, or yellow Ford would only be possible by using a combination of paint and varnish. A number of coats, a minimum of five, and as many as fifteen, would be required. The body would have to be dried between coats, and then sanded. It would take two or three weeks per body, and this was obviously out of the question. Ford customers got black Fords. Most Chev-

The 1924 Oldsmobile Model 30 Sports Touring Car.
GENERAL MOTORS

The interior of a Model T Ford. FORD ARCHIVES

The 1926 Model T touring car had four-wheel mechanical brakes.   FORD MOTOR COMPANY

rolet customers got black Chevrolets too, although there were some gray Chevrolets, and some in sort of pea-soup green. When a man showed up in a bright yellow Cadillac, it told the world that not only was he a sport, but that he had been willing to pay a large price for his yellow wagon.

Kettering, despite his genius, was a modest man. When his first attempts to develop a paint, which would dry within a couple of hours and offer some pleasant choices of color, failed, he admitted his failure and did the sensible thing. He asked DuPont to assign their chemists to the problem. He turned over what data he had collected, and DuPont scientists added it to their own fund of knowledge.

They had made one breakthrough in their attempts to do away with the paintbrush and long drying times. Brass beds were the height of fashion then, and they had a tendency to tarnish before they left the factory. DuPont scientists had developed a lacquer, composed essentially of liquified cotton, which could be sprayed through a nozzle, like water. It gave the brass bedsteads a thin, transparent covering which kept them from tarnishing.

It wasn't applicable to automobile bodies for two reasons, the most significant being that it was transparent. And the coat was too thin for the protection an auto body needed.

When they tried to make it thicker, it clogged up the paint nozzle. When they tried to put color in it, the solution came out of the nozzle like so many millions of tiny colored BB's.

139

*The 1928-9 Model A sedan.
The enclosed body was an
"extra cost" option.*
FORD MOTOR COMPANY

*By 1931, the open car (this is
a sport phaeton) was the
luxury, "extra cost" version.*
FORD MOTOR COMPANY

*A 1932 Ford V-8 roadster like
this one is worth about twice
as much money today—if not
more—than when it was new.*
FORD MOTOR COMPANY

But the germ of the solution obviously was there. Pressed hard by Boss Kettering (after all, he was a crony of Pierre S. DuPont himself, as well as of John Jacob Raskob) the experimenters continued, without any appreciable success.

In 1920, at the laboratory in Parlin, New Jersey, DuPont chemists were working on motion picture film improvements in the building next door to the one in which the chemists were working on paint. The film chemists mixed a batch of a cellulose formula and rolled a barrel full of it outside their laboratory so it could be taken somewhere else.

The electrical system broke down and the lights stayed out for three days, during which time the freshly mixed batch of cellulose material sat forgotten in the sun and chill of the night outside the laboratory.

When the lights went back on, and the chemists went back to work, one of the film chemists, in almost idle conversation with one of the paint chemists, suddenly remembered the barrel of cellulose. It was obviously ruined. So ruined that the paint chemist went over to look at it in pure curiosity, as men are prone to take a good look at a wrecked car.

Because it had been subjected to strong variations of temperature, both felt sure that what they would find would be a fifty-five gallon barrel of thick glop, a cellulose jelly. They found instead a light, syrupy mixture. The paint chemist stirred it around and then asked, since it was obviously of no further use to the film chemists, if it would be all right if the paint chemists just took it.

Four years later, Duco lacquer first appeared on an Oldsmobile. It was a light blue Oldsmobile, called "True Blue," and its color had been applied through a spray nozzle and then dried in *less* time than black enamel had required.

The paint chemists at DuPont obviously deserve the bulk of the credit for the invention of the paint. But if it had not been for Kettering, who not only insisted that it could be done, but applied pressure through others to keep the chemists at their labors, it's possible that it would not have been discovered until much later.

What else was there to the automobile?

Brakes: The first brakes were mechanical. The modification to this was brakes on all four wheels, still mechanical. Then they became hydraulically assisted. Finally they became hydraulic and power-assisted.

Transmissions: The clutch was replaced by an automatic transmission which, although changed, bore very obvious internal similarities to Henry Ford's planetary transmission on the Model T.

Engines: The engine grew, one small step after another, from a single cylinder to two cylinders on either side of the crankshaft. Then there was the V-12 and V-16 and even V-24, with the entire industry finally settling on the V-8 as the optimum answer (although Pontiac once tried half of a V-8 engine).

Bodies: The enclosed touring car was far more expensive than the open car, because the industry had not yet learned to stamp steel body parts. A closed car generally

The 1924 blue Duco-painted Oldsmobile.
GENERAL MOTORS

In 1932 Ford put out its first V-8 engine.
FORD ARCHIVES

The Dodge brothers, Horace (left) and John, in the rear of the first production Dodge, November 14, 1914.

DODGE MOTOR COMPANY

In this 1916 Dodge Brothers Touring Car, General John J. "Black Jack" Pershing chased the Mexican bandit, Pancho Villa. It is now in the West Point Museum.
  35 hp; @ 2,000 rpm;
  compression 4:1; 4-cylinder engine;
  wheel base 114 inches; displacement 212.3 inches.

DODGE MOTOR COMPANY

The 1917 Dodge Brothers three-door sedan.
  35 hp; @ 2,000 rpm;
  compression 4:1; 4-cylinder engine;
  wheel base 114 inches; displacement 212.3 inches.
                    DODGE MOTOR COMPANY

The 1931 Dodge Eight, five-passenger sedan. (In 1931,
"Brothers" was dropped from the firm name.)
  84 hp; @ 3,400 rpm;
  compression 5.4:1; 8-cylinder engine;
  wheelbase 118 inches; displacement 240.3 inches.
                    DODGE MOTOR COMPANY

The 1932 Dodge Eight. The ram was introduced as a radiator ornament, and jokesters said it memorialized the temperament of the founders.
   100 hp; @ 3,400 rpm;
compression 6.35:1; 8-cylinder engine;
wheelbase 122⅜ inches; displacement 282.1 inches.

DODGE MOTOR COMPANY

The 1934 Dodge Six. Eight-cylinder engines did not sell in this Depression year, and Dodge dropped them.
   87 hp; @ 3,600 rpm;
compression 6.5:1; 6-cylinder engine;
wheelbase 121 inches; displacement 217.8 inches.

DODGE MOTOR COMPANY

The 1940 Dodge Six four-door "Luxury Liner Deluxe."
87 hp; @ 3,600 rpm (same engine as before);
compression 6.5:1; 6-cylinder engine
wheelbase 119½ inches; displacement 217.8 inches.

DODGE MOTOR COMPANY

The 1941 Dodge Luxury Liner Custom.
"Improvements" advertised were a divided grill, a
one-piece hood, and lights on the fenders, as well as
four more horsepower gained by taking the reading at
3,800 rpm. The engine was just about identical to the
old one.
91 hp; @ 3,800 rpm;
compression 6.5:1; 6-cylinder engine;
wheelbase 119½ inches; displacement 217.8 inches.

DODGE MOTOR COMPANY

The 1950 Dodge Coronet.
   103 hp; @ 3,600 rpm;
   compression 7:1; 6-cylinder engine;
   wheelbase 123.5 inches; displacement 230.2 inches.

DODGE MOTOR COMPANY

The 1953 Dodge Coronet V-8.
   140 hp; @ 4,400 rpm;
   compression 7.1:1; 8-cylinder V-8 engine;
   wheelbase 119 inches; displacement 241.2 inches.

DODGE MOTOR COMPANY

The 1960 Dodge Polara V-8.
  330 hp; @ 4,400 rpm;
  compression 9:1; 8-cylinder V-8 engine;
  wheelbase 122 inches; displacement 361 inches.
                    DODGE MOTOR COMPANY

A 1969 Dodge Monaco four-door hardtop.
  330 hp; @ 5,000 rpm;
  compression 10:1; 8-cylinder V-8 engine;
  wheelbase 121 inches; displacement 383 inches.
                    DODGE MOTOR COMPANY

cost $500 more than an open one. But the people wanted closed cars, and gradually that price differential reversed itself as the industry learned how to make closed bodies. In 1922 Hudson and Essex reduced the difference to $100.

By the end of 1929, the difference not only was gone, but reversed. "Convertible touring cars" now commanded the premium price, as they do today.

In 1929, 5,337,087 cars were made in the United States. That record held until 1949. Now there are tears of sorrow in Detroit if 7,000,000 cars aren't bought each year, and the manufacturers look confidently toward the 8,000,000 car year.

The cold truth is that there really isn't much difference between the cars of 1929 and the cars of today. There have been steady improvements, so that cars go faster and more comfortably. Tires have been improved. Better steels and other metals and plastics have been developed. There is safety glass on the windows, and there are clever little signs and buzzers and alarms to help the driver stay awake and on the road, but in large measure, reduced to its basics, the following definition of a car is just as applicable to the shiniest thing on the showroom floor as it is to the pride of 1929:

An automobile consists of a rubber-tired chassis and body. An internal-combustion water-cooled engine operating on a petrocarbon fluid generates power which is delivered to the wheels through a transmission and differ-

ential. The vehicle is equipped with illuminating and warning lights and a number of devices for passenger comfort, such as heating and upholstered seats. The operator controls the vehicle with controls for acceleration, stopping, and turning. It is considered, by some, despite its obvious advantages, to be a menace to human life and health.

CHAPTER **X**   There is a television commercial which goes something like this: "If it's anything to do with fabrics, we do it, and we do more of it than anyone else."

While the commercial is probably true, the slogan, substituting "automobiles" for "fabrics" precisely fits the role of the United States.

"If it's anything to do with automobiles, America does it, and does more of it than the rest of the world combined."

Now it is true, of course, that there are major automobile manufacturers which have no financial connections with their American counterparts. Volkswagen comes immediately to mind.

Volkswagen means "people's car." It began as a government sponsored fraud in Nazi Germany. The people's car was to be bought on the installment plan by the German workingman. There was one significant difference between that installment plan and the one Americans are used to. In Hitler's Germany you made your payments, and when you made all of them, you were supposed to get your car—*after* it had been paid for, not before.

The thousands of people who faithfully made their payments before the war were to be disappointed. They didn't get their car. There was a Volkswagen, of sorts, a slab-sided, rear-air-cooled engine vehicle, but it was a sort of second-class jeep for Hitler's army, rather than a car for the people.

After the war, of course, the factory at Wolfsberg did begin to make the Volkswagen. It was designed by Dr.

Ferdinand Porsche, who readily admitted that he'd been very impressed with the Franklin air-cooled engine and had studied it in great detail before designing his own engine.

The Volkswagen was and is a great success. Its philosophy for almost twenty years has been not to have a new model every year, but rather to incorporate improvements as they are developed. In this way, production costs can be kept down, and more people are able to afford a car. The philosophy of the Volkswagen Company sounds as if it were copied word for word from Henry Ford.

Neither, of course, is Mercedes-Benz owned by American interests. That's pure German, tracing its ancestry all the way back to Daimler.

During World War II, when the first Americans reached the Rhine River at Cologne, they were somewhat astonished to capture a Rhine River Steamer named the Henry Ford. It belonged to Ford of Germany, whose plant had been leveled by B-24 Bombers built at the Ford-built-and-operated Willow Run Bomber Plant.

The plant was rebuilt after the war, and Ford of Germany is as powerful as it ever was, its Ford Taunus and other models competing with Volkswagen and Opel. Opel is owned by General Motors.

In France, the largest manufacturer of cars is Renault, which is owned by the French government. Right behind it, however, is Simca, which has strong connections with Chrysler. There is, of course, Ford of France.

The military Volkswagen of World War II. There were some 50,000 of these cars.   VOLKSWAGEN OF AMERICA

This is the Volkswagen hundreds of thousands of Germans paid for but few got. Only 1,785 were made before Germany lost the war, and most of them went to Nazi government officials.   VOLKSWAGEN OF AMERICA

Americans don't do too well in Italy, where Fiat is, by a large margin, the major manufacturer. The story is told and denied by Fiat, that the reason the Americans haven't really battled for a market in Italy is because they own a large part of Fiat and would be competing with themselves.

Ford of England is the largest manufacturer of automobiles in England.

Across the world in Australia, the most popular car is the Holden, owned by General Motors. Jeeps are built all around the world by companies either owned or operated by the Kaiser Jeep Corporation. In some parts of South America, Willys are still built from tools and dies shipped there from Detroit.

What about the Soviet Union and the Communist satellites? Last year, they had the best year, in terms of production, they had ever had, manufacturing a total of 728,000 motor vehicles (251,000 cars and the rest trucks and buses). The United States, during the same period (not counting what was made by U. S.-owned manufacturers outside the country) made well over 9,000,000 cars, trucks, and buses. Czechoslovakia made 112,000 passenger cars last year, East Germany 110,000, Yugoslavia 42,000, and Poland about 40,000.

If one particular model of a popularly priced American car doesn't sell 50,000, it is very often dropped from the line. That was the fate of the Chevrolet Corvair, 1959–1969.

According to the Ford Motor Company (we have so

The 1964 Chrysler turbine engine
passenger car. What looks like stop
lights are the turbine exhausts.

CHRYSLER CORPORATION

The Opel GT, manufactured in
Germany by Adam Opel, G.m.b.H.,
owned by General Motors, is sold in
the United States by Buick dealers.

GENERAL MOTORS

G M's answer to traffic congestion.
This two-passenger car has a 12-hp
aluminum engine. Top speed is 45
mph, range is 280 miles on four gallons
of gasoline (70 miles per gallon).

GENERAL MOTORS

many vehicles that counting them is quite a chore) there are about 96,000,000 vehicles of all sorts on American roads, more than 90 per cent of them owned by private citizens and businesses. In the Soviet Union, to serve a population roughly twice the size of ours, there are only 1,100,000 vehicles, and 90 per cent of these are owned by the Russian government. Alabama, with a population of about three and a half million people (one-one hundredth that of Russia) has about a quarter of a million *more* vehicles (1,455,883) of all sorts than does Russia. Twenty-eight of the fifty United States each have more vehicles than the Russians.

In 1965, Americans paid $4,175,972,000 in gasoline taxes. That's enough money to buy, at $4,000 each, all the vehicles on the roads of the Soviet Union. If we did buy every bus, truck, and passenger car in the Soviet Union, and figuring five people to each vehicle, they would only carry about half of the Americans licensed to drive cars.

There are almost as many cars in the United States as there are licensed drivers. New York State has 5,540,769 vehicles and 7,664,391 drivers for them. In less crowded states, the figures came closer. Texas, for example, has about 5,100,000 drivers to drive 5,060,000 vehicles; Illinois 4,870,000 drivers for 4,100,000 vehicles; and California has *more* vehicles (9,100,000) than drivers (9,050,000.) There are a total of 93,667,928 licensed drivers in the United States.

In something of an understatement, this is a mixed blessing.

The advantages to our economy are hard to conceive. It is said that one man in five earns his living in an industry connected with the automobile. Making steel for it, or rubber, or drilling for oil, pumping gas, financing new cars, making material for seat covers, paving roads, serving as a policeman, and so on almost indefinitely.

The automobile, on the other hand, is responsible for more accidental deaths than anything in our society, generally causing twenty times as many deaths as the often-maligned firearm, twice as many as falls, five times as many as burns, seven times as many as drowning, twenty times as many as the railroads, and fifteen times as many deaths as poison gases and other poisons put together.

They are by far the most dangerous form of transportation. For every hundred million miles traveled, 2.3 people are killed in a car. If you go by bus, your chances of survival are precisely ten times greater.

Airlines are even safer, with a record just about twice as good as busses. They lose only .12 passenger per one hundred million miles travelled. Safest of all (if you can find one that's still running), are the railroads, who lose only .07 passengers per hundred million passenger miles.

And cars are a relatively inefficient means of transportation. A car capable of carrying six people 130 mph on the highways being used to carry only the driver at five miles per hour through the traffic of midtown New York might be laughable, if the machine weren't also pouring out noxious and poisonous fumes from its exhaust into the air as it crawls along.

158

The gasoline engine and the car it propels aren't entirely to blame, of course. Industry does its share to poison our air, aided and abetted by the leaf and garbage burners in every town. But the fumes from burned and partially consumed gasoline are, without doubt, a serious and growing problem all over the United States.

The car itself is getting to be a major disposal problem. In other parts of the world, the custom is to keep making repairs so the car can be used until it can be repaired no more. Not so in this country. We make so many, and we make them so cheaply (primarily in terms of efficient utilization of labor) that it soon reaches the point where it's cheaper to get another car than to fix the one you have.

New York City has to haul away two hundred or more abandoned cars each week, and the figures run proportionately the same across the country. It isn't as if they're used up. If they were used up, they wouldn't pose so much of a problem. But only a very tiny fraction of their weight has been worn off by use. A junk car weighs just about as much as it did when it came off the assembly line.

Engineers have developed huge hydraulic presses which reduce a car to a cube of metal three feet square. That reduces the space problem somewhat, but the weight is still there. Other machines have been developed which literally grind old cars to bits, as cheese is grated in the kitchen. Some coast communities, solving two problems at once, haul them off shore and drop them overboard to build artificial reefs.

(left) Ford's "Floating Sponge" oil skimmer, being lowered into the water at River Rouge.
(right) Ford operates this "Floating Sponge" at its River Rouge plant twenty-four hours a day to clear oil and debris from the river.

FORD MOTOR COMPANY

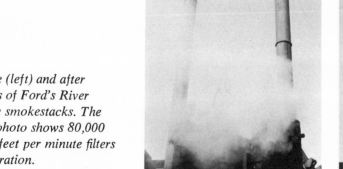

Before (left) and after photos of Ford's River Rouge smokestacks. The right photo shows 80,000 cubic feet per minute filters in operation.

FORD MOTOR COMPANY

Far too many cars are simply taken to an open field to rust and become an eyesore.

Making the cars, and the parts that go into them, is a dirty business, partly because it's such a huge industry, and uses large quantities of raw material and leaves large quantities of waste.

The manufacturers are aware of this problem, and, on their own, as well as under steadily increasing government prodding, and in response to a growing public awareness of contaminated air and water, have taken major steps to reduce or entirely eliminate pollution.

It's not easy.

Ford's River Rouge plant, near Dearborn, Michigan, for example, takes 400,000,000 gallons of water each day from the Detroit River, uses it in all sorts of manufacturing processes, and returns it to the river. Not only does Ford have to concern itself with returning clean water to the river after it uses it, for both ethical and legal reasons, but it has to worry about what someone else has done to the water before it reaches the Ford intake culverts. Ford can't use dirty water any more than anyone else can.

In 1966 Ford set aside $80,000,000 for air and water pollution control for its plants in the United States. Other money was set aside for Ford plants around the world.

It cost Ford $3,500,000 to install electrical dust collectors at the River Rouge plant powerhouse. Microscopic particles of dust and carbon which formerly went up in the air as smoke are now trapped and kept from polluting the air. At the Iron Foundry (where, for exam-

Prototype small cars from General Motors: (top) the 511, three-wheel; (bottom) 512 hybrid gasoline-electric; (right, top) 512 pure electric; and (right, bottom) 512 gasoline engine car.

GENERAL MOTORS

ple, engine blocks are cast) Ford installed a dust collector costing $4,300,000. The largest dust collectors in the world trap waste at Ford's Basic Oxygen Furnace, where steel is made.

The National Wildlife Foundation, dedicated not only to preserving the cleanliness of the atmosphere, but also to cleaning it up when it's being polluted, is an organization with a reputation for its willingness to take on any offender, from the U. S. Government on down. In 1967 it cited the Ford Motor Company as the "industrial leader in the elimination of air and water pollution."

This, of course, inspired the competition to increase their efforts. It isn't simply a question of spending money, but more of finding techniques of manufacture that are less dirty than those currently in use, or of finding better and more efficient filtering and disposal systems for the waste that is inescapable. Cyanide, a deadly poison, for example, is a by-product of the manufacture of coke, which in turn is needed to make steel. Ford found a complicated way of disposing of the cyanide. It was collected and then fed back into the gases which fueled the coke ovens, destroying a large part of it. But there is still some left over, and cyanide gas is so lethal that California uses it in its gas chamber. So Ford had next to develop a filter and collector to fit into the smokestacks of the coke furnace. It took a lengthy and expensive period of experimentation before the problem was solved.

But while the industry is, by its own admission, a large source of pollution, it is the product of the industry, the shiny, chrome-bedecked, gasoline-burning automobile, which causes about 90 per cent of the pollution.

In early 1967, recognizing their mutual obligation to do something about reducing exhaust-pipe pollution, Ford and Mobil Oil Corporation formed the Inter-Industry Emission Control Program. Mobil's competitors, Sun Oil, Marathon Oil, Atlantic-Richfield, American Oil, and Standard Oil (Ohio) soon joined the group.

(Other manufacturers are conducting their own programs, either separately, or in connection with other oil producers.)

In 1968, recognizing that as their countries began to put a car in everybody's garage, they were going to have the same sort of problems we have, Fiat of Italy, Mitsubishi Industries, Nissan Motors, and Toyo Kogyo of Japan, applied for, and were granted membership in the Inter-Industry Emission Control Program.

Each automobile really gives off relatively few contaminants. But when even a very small figure is multiplied by 96,000,000, the number of vehicles on the road, the result is a vast quantity of dirty fumes.

The contaminants are carbon monoxide, hydrocarbons, and oxides of nitrogen. Most of them come from the combustion process—the burning of fuel in engine cylinders. Carbon monoxide and the hydrocarbons are the result of incompletely burned fuel.

It's possible, for an engine that runs always at the same speed, to develop a fuel mixture and an exhaust filtering system that will just about completely eliminate the prob-

163

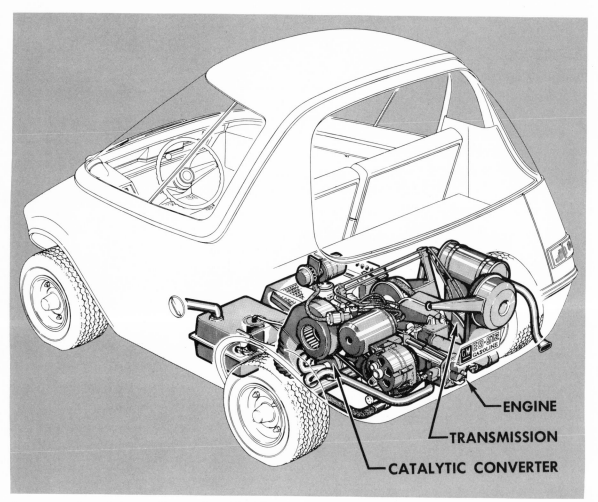

ENGINE

TRANSMISSION

CATALYTIC CONVERTER

A cutaway view of the gasoline engine, GM 212
commuter. The catalytic converter removes
hydrocarbons from the exhaust.

GENERAL MOTORS

lem. But car engines don't run at constant speeds; indeed, it's rare when they run at same rate for more than a few seconds at a time.

A fuel mixture that would just about completely burn up the fuel at 3,000 rpm, will not run the same engine at 5,000, and at 1,500 rpm will pour unburned fuel into the atmosphere. Engineers have had to develop a fuel system which, first of all, will alter the fuel/air mixture as engine speed changes. They admit they cannot do this perfectly, and hence, unburned fuel will continue to enter the exhaust system.

One source of contaminants which does not enter the exhaust system is the unburned gases in the cylinder which, instead of being vented out the exhaust valve, force their way past the piston rings and go into the crankcase. For years these gases were simply discharged under the car. Since 1963, the gases have been fed from the crankcase to the intake manifold, where they were mixed with gasoline and air, and then burned in the cylinder. This reduced pollution by hydrocarbons by about 15 per cent.

Other solutions are being tested. One of these involves the catalyst principle. A catalyst is an element which, when brought into contact with some other elements, chemically changes them, while remaining unchanged itself. When a catalyst is brought into contact with some pollutants, it changes them chemically into harmless substances. The problem here is that catalysts are very expensive (one of the best is platinum) and that the tetra-

165

ethyl lead which increases the octane rating of gas quickly reduces the effectiveness of a catalyst.

Another solution being tested is an "afterburner." After the fuel is passed through the engine to extract its energy, the exhaust (containing some unburned fuel) would be passed through another combustion chamber, the sole purpose of which would be to complete burning up the fuel.

So far, neither program has been completely successful.

It was determined in 1963 that new cars were discharging into the atmosphere 900 parts per million of hydrocarbons and 3.5 per cent (by volume) of carbon monoxide. The government stepped in and announced that this was wholly unsatisfactory, and that if the manufacturers wanted to sell any 1968 automobiles, they must have engines and exhaust systems which reduced the 900 parts per million of hydrocarbon to 275, and the percentage by volume of carbon monoxide from 3.5 to 1.5.

At the same time, the government announced that by 1970, manufacturers would be required to reduce the hydrocarbons to one-fifth (180 parts per million) of the 1963 levels, and the carbon monoxide emissions to 1 per cent by volume, less than one-third of the 1963 levels.

It is the goal of the Inter-Industry Emission Control Program, and of the scientists from Tokyo to Detroit to Turin who are now working around the clock, to reduce emission to a low of 65 hydrocarbon parts per million, and carbon monoxide to .03 per cent by volume.

CHAPTER IX

Since they are in the business of selling gasoline-powered automobiles, the manufacturers understandably are reluctant to come out and publicly announce the obvious solution to air-poisoning by the gasoline engine: Get rid of the gasoline engine.

On the other hand, every member of the industry is actively engaged in trying to do just that. And in fairness, it must be said that the attempt to find a substitute for the gasoline engine, and its emissions, had been going on long before the public outcry against air pollution began.

Edward N. Cole, President of General Motors, had some interesting comments on the subject to make on May 7, 1969, interesting because of what was said, and who said them. The ideas and intentions of the president of the largest corporation in the world are bound to affect the lives of everybody.

Mr. Cole divided the development of the automobile into six eras. The first, he said, lasted two hundred years, from the development of gunpowder (and the idea of the piston) to Otto's Silent Gas Engine in 1876. The second era, Cole said, was the experimental period, the twenty-five years from 1876–1900. Next, stabilization 1900–1925; mass production 1925–1945; and refinement, 1945–1960. The sixth—and current—era began in 1960. The GM chief executive called it the era of "power train optimization."

"Optimization" is one of those large, many-syllable

words so popular with big corporations and the government. Freely translated, what Mr. Cole was saying is that we are now in the era of development of the best power train. In other words, we will, in this era, develop highly efficient transmissions to send power from an engine that is either a greatly improved gasoline internal-combustion engine, or a turbine, or some other sort of power plant.

Cole said that in the past forty years, General Motors has experimented with "just about every type and configuration of power plant that could possibly compete with the gasoline internal-combustion engine." He mentioned electric power plants, steam engines, free piston engines, diesel and gas turbines, and hybrid power plants. Hybrids are a combination of two kinds of engines. For example, a gasoline engine hooked to an electrical generator, or a battery charger, so that electric power, rather than a mechanical connection to the gasoline engine, would actually turn the wheels.

All of these, he said, have advantages, either real or potential, over the gasoline engine, and all of them seem to be capable of reducing air pollution. But none of them, he said, can replace the gasoline engine in all its present-day applications.

There have been major developments, for example, in storage batteries. Science has developed batteries that are lighter than the wet-acid batteries they will replace. The batteries are smaller, more powerful, have longer life, and can be charged far more easily and far more often than other batteries.

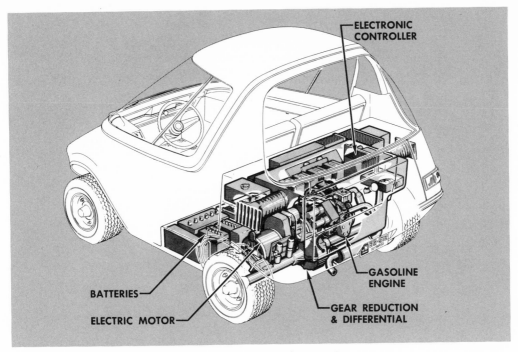

A cutaway view of the GM 512 hybrid. The gasoline engine charges the batteries; the batteries, in turn, power the motor. GENERAL MOTORS

A cutaway view of the pure electric GM 212. GENERAL MOTORS

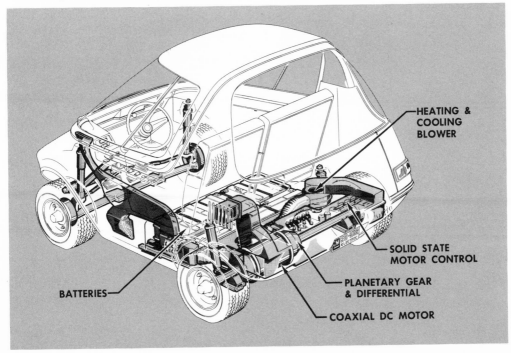

But none of this changes the basic rules of physics which say that so many volts are required to move a car weighing so many pounds over a given distance. A battery-driven car—no matter how much money is spent on it— cannot, in what designers call "the present state of the art" go out on the highway, accelerate as fast as a gasoline-powered car, run at 70 mph for three hours, and then turn around and run 70 mph for three hours going home.

Even the new batteries won't permit this. High speed quickly drains a battery-stored power.

But there may be a place for battery-powered cars. Cities, for example, are plagued by automobiles for a number of reasons. Cars are too large, for one thing. They generate noxious fumes with their gasoline engines. A battery-powered car providing space for two people and a small amount of luggage would have a number of advantages in a city, where distances (compared to super highways) are short between stops, and where high speed is not only illegal but unnecessary. Two battery-powered cars of the size already built by General Motors and Ford would fit in the parking space now required for one full-sized car. It would be easy in the city to make provisions to recharge electric car batteries at, for example, regular gas stations. Electric cars would absolutely eliminate all air pollutants associated with gas and diesel cars.

On the other hand, cross-country trucks and buses, operating along super highways at fairly constant, high speeds, can efficiently use turbine power, which, under those conditions, produces energy with a very low level of air pollution. Turbines are not adaptable to the slow speed, and stop-and-go driving conditions of the city.

General Motors will make available in 1971 turbine-powered heavy trucks. It is expected that they will be put to use in the Western part of the country, where their particular characteristics will make them more valuable than gasoline or diesel engines.

General Motors, which has gone so far as to install a steam engine in a 1969 Pontiac, does not feel the steam engine is the answer, either.

Mr. Cole summed up the GM position by saying that the gasoline internal-combustion engine is today, as it was in 1900, the most feasible, practical, and best solution to powering road vehicles, and that it will remain the main power plant until such time as "major technological breakthroughs occur."

He didn't seem to hold out much hope for such breakthroughs, and he certainly should know what he's talking about.

Chrysler engineers began investigating the turbine some time before World War II. In 1945, the Navy gave Chrysler a contract to develop a turbine propeller (turbo-prop) engine for aircraft. When that program was discontinued, after the jet had proved itself, Chrysler engineers went back to their original intention of developing a turbine to replace the automobile and truck engine.

In 1954, they succeeded in building a turbine engine developing 100 hp, and small enough to fit in the engine

CUTAWAY VIEW OF GM SE-101 STEAM CAR

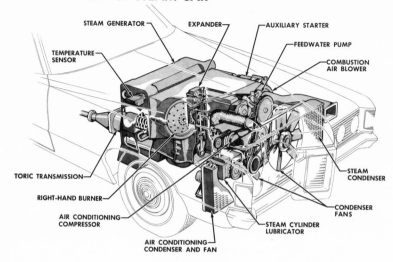

A cutaway view of the GM SE-101 steam engine in a 1969 Pontiac. GENERAL MOTORS

A cutaway view of a Beseler Engineering Company steam engine built for GM and installed in a 1969 Pontiac. GENERAL MOTORS

CUTAWAY VIEW OF GM SE-124 STEAM CAR WITH BESLER ENGINE

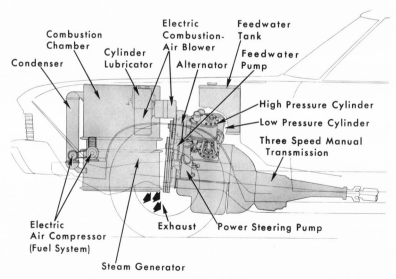

compartment of a 1954 Plymouth two-door. They had then at least partially tamed, if not whipped, one of the major disadvantages of the turbine engine—the fiery exhaust. With a heat exchanger, or regenerator, they extracted the heat from the exhaust gases, and used it to heat the air going into the turbine. This had the added advantage of lightening the job the turbine burner had to do, since it received hot air to start with.

When the car was moving, the temperature from the exhaust was less than 500° Fahrenheit (it had been 1200°F). At idle, the temperature was down to 170 degrees, less than that of boiling water.

Two years later, in 1956, Chrysler felt confident enough about its experimental engine to install it in a 1956 Plymouth, and run it coast to coast along the public highways. The results of the trip weren't spectacular. Using unleaded gasoline, it averaged 13 miles per gallon, which was hardly cause for joy. The significance was that it had gone that far without any major breakdown. The engine went back to the laboratory for further modification, and a version of it reappeared in 1959, mounted in another new car. Horsepower was up to about two hundred, and fuel consumption ranged as high as 18 miles per gallon.

The next year, Chrysler moved toward the General Motors position. A substantially identical engine was installed in a Dodge truck. It worked well, and development moved along now in two lines, one for passenger cars and the other for heavy-duty vehicles.

Installing GM's SE-101 steam engine in a 1969 Pontiac Grand Prix. GENERAL MOTORS

173

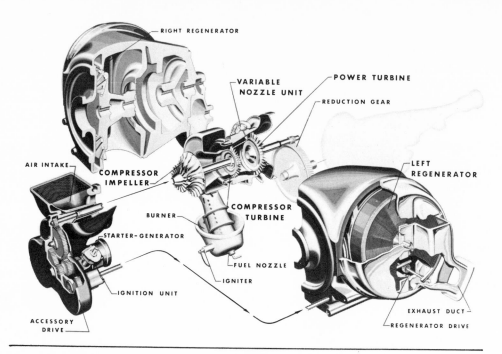

RIGHT REGENERATOR

VARIABLE NOZZLE UNIT

POWER TURBINE

REDUCTION GEAR

AIR INTAKE

COMPRESSOR IMPELLER

LEFT REGENERATOR

COMPRESSOR TURBINE

BURNER

FUEL NOZZLE

STARTER-GENERATOR

IGNITER

IGNITION UNIT

ACCESSORY DRIVE

EXHAUST DUCT

REGENERATOR DRIVE

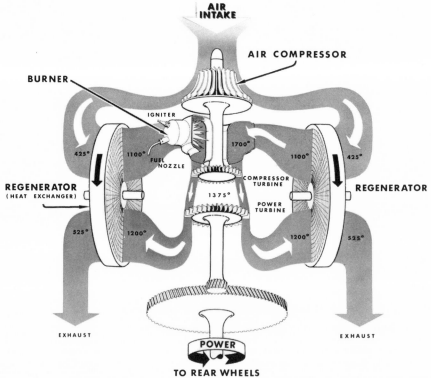

AIR INTAKE

AIR COMPRESSOR

BURNER

IGNITER

425°

1700°

1100°

425°

REGENERATOR (HEAT EXCHANGER)

1100°

FUEL NOZZLE

COMPRESSOR TURBINE

REGENERATOR

1375°

POWER TURBINE

525°

1200°

1200°

525°

EXHAUST

EXHAUST

POWER

TO REAR WHEELS

(top) Cutaway view of Chrysler passenger car turbine engine.
(bottom) How the Chrysler passenger turbine engine works.

CHRYSLER CORPORATION

Two 1962 Dodge Darts, one right from the assembly line, and the other powered with a turbine, left New York City on December 27, 1961, and drove to Los Angeles. The turbine provided better mileage, with lower quality fuel, than the standard vehicle.

A Plymouth was equipped with a turbine, and the Dodge and the Plymouth were sent around the country on the major test, the one that really counted: "Would you buy this car if it were on sale?" Of the people who saw it, 30 per cent said they'd buy, and 54 per cent said they'd think seriously about it. The remaining 16 per cent said that it was a menace on the road, like the horseless carriage, and that they wouldn't buy it at any price.

The Society of Mechanical Engineers broke a long standing rule that year. For the first time in their history, they gave an award to an automotive engineer. George J. Heubner, Jr., Chrysler's Research Executive Engineer received the award for the "development of the first automotive gas turbine engine suitable for mass production passenger automobiles."

Chrysler was enthusiastic. They established a production line for turbine cars, and Chrysler's president, Lynn Townsend, posed proudly with it. Fifty cars were built. They were loaned to a total of 203 people who had expressed interest in the turbine car by writing to Chrysler, and at least one car was sent to every state, plus the District of Columbia. Almost without exception (there being a few soreheads in every group of two hundred people) the drivers expressed admiration for the car, and said they would be willing to buy one if they were on sale.

They weren't. The cars were returned to Chrysler and disassembled for inspection. It was reported that the cars had held up remarkably well in the hands of the public. A whole new era dawned. The turbine car had no need of high-test gasoline, or even of regular gasoline. It could be run on diesel fuel. Or on kerosene. Or fuel oil. If you happened to be near an airport, you could fuel it with JP-4, the same fuel used in the Pratt & Whitney jets on a DC-9.

Mr. Townsend posed again in 1964 with the first customer, Mr. Richard E. Vlaha, of Broadview, Illinois, and the cameras clicked as Mr. Vlaha became the first customer to take possession of a turbine-powered automobile.

From that point on, however, the sound of the trumpets has been somewhat muted. The Chrysler Corporation is no longer selling any turbine-powered automobiles. It is rather shy when asked when it plans to put them on sale again, and just about as shy when asked why they were taken off the market. It would appear that Chrysler hasn't solved the problems that go with changing a power plant yet, either. At least not for passenger cars.

Ford began work on turbine engines in 1952. By 1954, they had built an engine developing 150-shaft hp. It was small enough to fit in a 1954 Ford engine compartment and had a regenerator. The turbine apparently posed the same problems to Ford that it posed to Chrysler, but Ford had less enthusiasm. After that one quick shot at a passenger-car engine, Ford devoted the great majority of

176

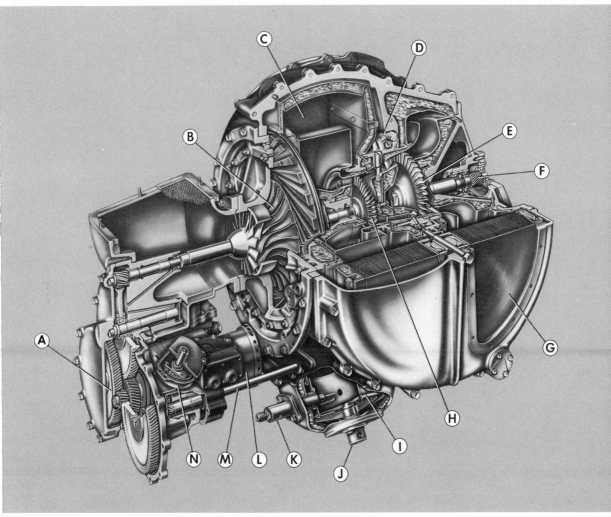

*The Chrysler passenger car turbine engine.
(A) accessory drive; (B) compresser impeller, which
draws air in and compresses it; (C) right regenerator
rotor, which uses heat from exhaust gases to heat
incoming air; (D) variable nozzle, provides engine
braking, and permits economical use of fuel; (E) power
turbine, which drives rear wheels; (F) 10:1 reduction
gear; (G) right regenerator rotor; (H) first-stage turbine;
(I) burner, where fuel burns at 1700°F; (J) fuel nozzle;
(K) fuel igniter; (L) starter-generator; (M) regenerator
driveshaft; (N) ignition unit.* CHRYSLER CORPORATION

ENGINE SIZE COMPARISON
GAS TURBINE vs. CONVENTIONAL

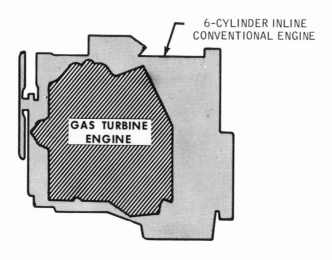

6-CYLINDER INLINE
CONVENTIONAL ENGINE

GAS TURBINE
ENGINE

REGENERATIVE GAS TURBINE ENGINE

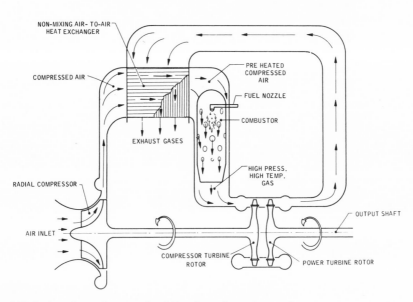

NON-MIXING AIR- TO-AIR
HEAT EXCHANGER

COMPRESSED AIR

PRE HEATED
COMPRESSED
AIR

FUEL NOZZLE

COMBUSTOR

EXHAUST GASES

HIGH PRESS.
HIGH TEMP.
GAS

RADIAL COMPRESSOR

OUTPUT SHAFT

AIR INLET

COMPRESSOR TURBINE
ROTOR

POWER TURBINE ROTOR

*(top) Relative sizes of a standard Ford truck engine and
a turbine engine which replaces it.
(bottom) How the Ford truck turbine engine works.*

FORD MOTOR COMPANY

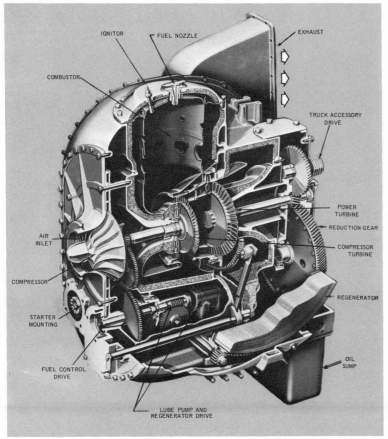

IGNITOR FUEL NOZZLE EXHAUST

COMBUSTOR

TRUCK ACCESSORY
DRIVE

POWER
TURBINE

REDUCTION GEAR

AIR
INLET

COMPRESSOR
TURBINE

COMPRESSOR

REGENERATOR

STARTER
MOUNTING

OIL
SUMP

FUEL CONTROL
DRIVE

LUBE PUMP AND
REGENERATOR DRIVE

*A cutaway view of a Ford turbine
truck engine.*

FORD MOTOR COMPANY

*A Ford truck turbine engine
installed in a standard Ford heavy
truck (left) is one ton lighter and
two-thirds the size of the standard
gasoline engine (right) it replaces.
Both develop about 375 hp.*

FORD MOTOR COMPANY

its efforts toward turbine power for trucks. By 1966, Ford had developed a 375-hp turbine, suitable for use in its heaviest trucks.

Ford is still "some years" away from producing turbines for commercial use, but it seems to be simply a question of time until turbines are in use, and it's not stretching the imagination too much to conceive that truck-engine experience may well result in knowledge leading to a successful turbine for passenger cars as well.

Ford has also done a great deal of work—much of it in England, where road crowding is getting to be more of a problem than it is here—with small, battery-powered, gasoline-powered, and hybrid gas-electric vehicles for the future.

And, almost predictably, there is a new name on the horizon, William P. Lear, a man who would have been perfectly at home with Daimler and Benz, with Peugeot and Rolls, with Ford, Durant, Kettering and Sloan.

Mr. Lear is a character, as well as an inventive genius. He made his first fortune in electronics, by developing communication and navigation equipment for aircraft.

Some years ago, after a series of disputes with European customs officials at various airports, and after being told that it was simply out of the question for a private American citizen to fly his own airplane to Russia, Lear thought—and proved—he had the solution to this problem.

He equipped himself with a uniform. Or what looked like a uniform. He selected from various uniforms those

The Comuta chassis, showing battery placement.
FORD MOTOR COMPANY

A cutaway view of the Ford of England battery-powered "Comuta."

FORD MOTOR COMPANY

The Ford of England battery-powered Comuta with a Mustang.

FORD MOTOR COMPANY

features (gold braid and so on) which he thought made the wearer look most important, and instructed a tailor to incorporate them on a uniform for him. For the basic color of the uniform, he selected a very light blue.

He loaded Mrs. Lear into his twin-engined private airplane and set off for Moscow. European airport personnel are very status conscious, as well as uniform conscious, and it apparently was beyond the comprehension of any European customs official that a private American citizen, flying his own airplane, would show up in such a splendid uniform. There was saluting and bowing and scraping, and speeches of welcome whereever the Lears touched down, including Moscow.

Our own State Department was less than overjoyed. Not only had Lear successfully made the trip to Moscow in his private plane, which they had publicly announced was absolutely impossible, but they were afraid the Russians would grab the airplane which, of course, was fully equipped with the latest Lear-designed navigation and communications equipment, conceded to be at least five years ahead of the Russians. Lear returned from Russia without incident, grandly returning the salutes he was tossed by Russian airport officials.

At the time Lear went into the airplane business, it was absolutely agreed within and without the industry that the day of the individual entering the airplane business was over, as it was over for the individual trying to enter the automobile business. It had grown too large for one man to try to compete.

Lear announced he was going into the airplane business, and that he was going the build a jet airplane for private use, to be owned and operated by industry and whoever else happened to have a million dollars and wanted his own jet.

This time Lear had bitten off too much, said the experts. For one thing, designing and building a jet was simply out of the question for someone who had no real experience along those lines, and someone without a large engineering and manufacturing facility behind him just couldn't do it. Jets were so complicated and so expensive that even Douglas and Boeing approached a new model very carefully. Since Cessna and Beech (the largest manufacturers of private aircraft) had considered a jet and discarded the idea as being wholly impractical (once they built it, who would buy it?) it was generally agreed that Lear was going to wind up sad and broke.

Lear built his jet. He found a market for it all over the world. (Frank Sinatra formed a company to buy several of them, which he rented out to people in the motion picture and other industries when he wasn't using one of them himself.) And the jet is still going strong, although Lear sold out this company too.

He had a new idea, and since no one else apparently was going to do anything about it, he would. He formed the Lear-Reno Corporation at what had been Stead Air Force Base in Reno, Nevada, and announced he was going to build an engine to replace the internal-combustion gasoline engine.

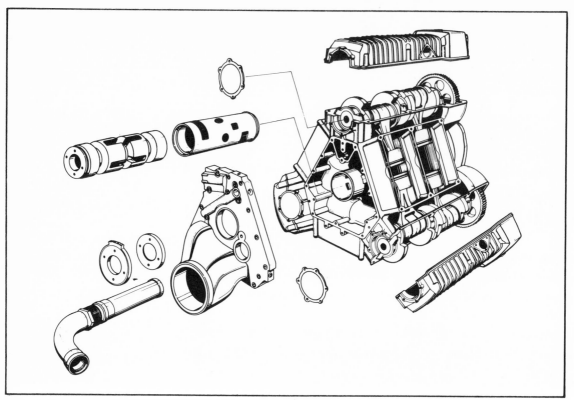

The Lear 600 hp external combustion engine.
LEAR MOTORS CORPORATION

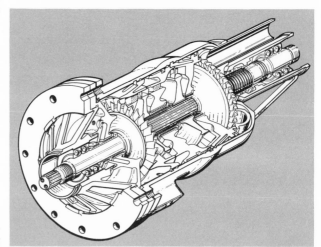

A cutaway view of the Lear turbine.
LEAR MOTORS CORPORATION

"The fact is," says Lear, "that if automobiles continue in their present direction of development, in the not too distant future, the air we breathe will be polluted to the point where it will be unfit to support human life. This is not just a possibility, it's a fact."

He rather bluntly told General Motors, Ford, Chrysler, and the rest of the industry where they've all gone wrong:

"What they have ignored is the cause of the problem. The internal-combustion engine burns fuel very rapidly in immediate contact with a cylinder wall, under circumstances in which complete combustion cannot possibly occur."

He dismissed the electric car, the hybrid, and just about everything else by saying, "Steam . . . or possibly the turbine . . . is the only answer."

He has already built both a triangular 600-hp *external* combustion motor (to be driven by steam) and his own turbine. He recently announced that he's ready to build engines, using what he calls the closed cycle system, which will "double the horsepower in one-third the displacement, and with less than one half the weight" of engines currently in use.

Established industry laughed at Henry Ford and William C. Durant too and neither of them made anything like the $100,000,000 or so that Bill Lear has already made doing things people said simply can't be done.

There may yet be a seventh era to add to the development of the self-propelled vehicle, the era of the external-combustion motor.

INDEX

189

DATE DUE

MAY 1 '79			
MAY 2 3 2010			
GAYLORD			PRINTED IN U.S.A.